ALL EARTH IS WAITING

Devotions for the Season

Katie Z. Dawson

Abingdon Press / Nashville

All Earth Is Waiting
Devotions for the Season

Copyright © 2017 Abingdon Press
All rights reserved.

No part of this work may be reproduced or transmitted in any form or by any means, electronic or mechanical, including photocopying and recording, or by any information storage or retrieval system, except as may be expressly permitted by the 1976 Copyright Act or in writing from the publisher. Requests for permission can be addressed to Permissions, The United Methodist Publishing House, PO Box 280988, 2222 Rosa L. Parks Blvd., Nashville, TN 37228-0988 or e-mailed to permissions@umpublishing.org.

This book is printed on elemental chlorine-free paper.
Library of Congress Cataloging-in-Publication data has been requested.
ISBN 978-1-5018-48070

Scripture quotations unless noted otherwise are taken from the Common English Bible, copyright 2011. Used by permission. All rights reserved.

Scripture quotations marked MSG are taken from THE MESSAGE, copyright © 1993, 1994, 1995, 1996, 2000, 2001, 2002 by Eugene H. Peterson. Used by permission of NavPress. All rights reserved. Represented by Tyndale House Publishers, Inc.

17 18 19 20 21 22 23 24 25 26 — 10 9 8 7 6 5 4 3 2 1
MANUFACTURED IN THE UNITED STATES OF AMERICA

CONTENTS

Week Three: Discovering Joy in the Abundance of the Earth

Week Four: The Peace of the World's Creatures

Introduction

The whole creation waits breathless with anticipation for the revelation of God's sons and daughters.

(Romans 8:19)

When Monsigeur Alberto Taulé sat down to compose music, he did so believing that "quality music and regular introduction of new songs are vital to a parish's spiritual health."[1] Not only was he a pastor, he also had a background in sacred music. And so in the wake of Vatican II, he began writing songs for Spanish-speaking churches all across the world. He wanted to help them sing their faith in new ways, believing that an unchanging collection of songs was unhealthy. He continued to write new music for a variety of church seasons until the year he died, including the hymn that we draw upon for the title of this devotional and accompanying study: "Toda la Tierra" ("All Earth Is Waiting").

That's one of the reasons I wanted to push beyond the familiar Advent hymns and texts during this particular season. Sometimes we find ourselves in a rut, believing that we already know the story and the promises of this time of year. And yet, those comforting traditional stories can lose their impact when we repeat them over and over again. The radical words of the prophets become dull. The longing for a new creation is appeased. The real problems of today are glossed over. New ideas about this season, new ways to encounter the longing of Advent, are vital to our spiritual health.

Advent is not simply about fondly recalling a past promise, but it is about the active longing for Christ to come again to redeem and restore the whole of creation. This unique double focus reminds us that we live between the "already" and the "not yet," and in the meantime we must be faithful with what God has placed in our care. Each of the weekly themes in this devotional calls us to recognize the breathless anticipation of the cosmos and our responsibility for its well-being. As we reflect upon the wonders of creation, sometimes we will be moved to confession and repentance and sometimes to a deeper commitment to be stewards of this world. For we are reminded that even as the earth waits "to see the Promised One," as Taulé's hymn says, God's presence is felt "throughout the earth today, / for he lives in all Christians and is with us now; / again, with his coming he brings us liberty."[2]

As the sons and daughters of God, we are a source of hope for all creation. Our first week's devotions invite us to consider how creation care is central to the Christian faith. In the second week of Advent, we will explore how we can be better stewards of the resources God has given us. Our third week's readings focus on what it means to celebrate the gifts of the creation, with particular attention to the plants and food that sustain us. Finally, we will dive into the circle of life and how visions of the peaceable kingdom impact our care for the creatures of this world.

These daily devotions are meant to accompany weekly Bible study. The selected Scriptures invite us to consider how that longing for the new creation and Christ's return should impact how we care for the world around us today. You are invited to start each week's devotions on Monday so the final reading of the week will fall on each of the Sundays of Advent.

Let us experience together how all earth is waiting for the Promised One.

1. "Alberto Taulé," Oregon Catholic Press, https://www.ocp.org/en-us /artists/339#bio. Accessed July 17, 2017.
2. Alberto Taulé, trans. by Gertrude C. Suppe, "All Earth Is Waiting," *The United Methodist Hymnal* (Nashville: The United Methodist Publishing House, 1989) 210, stanzas 1 and 4.

Week One

Creation Care and the Hope of Advent

1

Supremely Good

When God began to create the heavens and the earth....
God saw everything he had made: it was supremely good.
(Genesis 1:1, 31)

As Advent begins in my corner of the world, the leaves have fallen off the trees and the gardens are empty and dormant. Everything has been put away for the season and I am reminded of those first verses in Genesis where, "the earth was without shape or form" (Genesis 1:2). There is a quiet here and infinite possibility. As this Advent journey begins, I invite you into that space of reflection and stillness and hope for what could be born in the midst of this time.

I often use this season to ask what I have learned in my garden (and in my life) during the past year. I take time to remember what didn't work or where I struggled, and I allow those lessons to shape what comes next. I think about the landscape, the life, the faith I am trying to create. Surrounded by a world of dull browns, sometimes I open up the sleek pages of seed catalogs, dreaming about the spring. When I see the vibrant colors of a new variety of pepper or flower, I get itchy to add to the diversity of my garden and delight in the goodness of each individual item. Yet, one of the things I have discovered is that a garden doesn't thrive just because you fill it with good things.

You have to carefully plan the role every fruit, vegetable, and herb has in the space. Not every plant is a good neighbor, and sometimes their interactions can be harmful. I have to consider carefully how those many good things can benefit one another. Last season, I planted pumpkins in the middle of my summer squash and zucchini. But they competed too much for the same resources, and the pumpkins won. I created a large border of marigolds, both for the visual impact and to keep the bugs and rabbits away. But I learned, too late, that beans do not make good companions for marigolds and despite being protected from the rabbits, they failed to grow.

I have come to appreciate the importance of companion planting in my garden and how even flowers have a role in bringing out the best of various plants. Each in and of itself is good, but taken all together in a well-planned and careful way . . . well, that's when it is really good. As each element and plant is created in the first chapter of Genesis, God calls them good. And they are each put in just the right spot, at just the right time, with just the right purpose. When we reflect upon the complicated interweaving of life on this planet and the interaction of every plant, animal, grain of sand, and drop of water, it is truly amazing. Each remarkable creation is enhanced by its relationship with the others, and the result is greater than simply the sum of their parts. No wonder God looks out upon everything that was made and calls it *supremely good!*

You and I were given a particular role in God's masterpiece. We were invited to be caretakers and to fill this earth with life and abundance. While we might imagine that we are prized and honored above all of the other creations, the truth is that our goodness and value lie in how well we live out the role given to us. This Advent, we have an opportunity to reflect upon whether we have been good companions for the other creatures on this earth. As we stand on a threshold of new creation, we have a chance to learn from our mistakes and make new choices in light of the future we seek. Let us plan our gardens and our lives well, seeking always the hope of abundance that is found in God's supremely good creation.

Master Gardener of the world, everything you have made has a purpose and a place. Help us to delight in the interactions of your world and to cherish the goodness of creation. Remind us of the role to which you call us in this complicated web of life. Amen.

2

Creator of the Stars of Night

Heaven is declaring God's glory;
*   the sky is proclaiming his handiwork.*
One day gushes the news to the next,
*   and one night informs another what needs to be known.*

                                              (Psalm 19:1-2)

Long before I heard the call to pastoral ministry, I wanted to be a meteorologist. My collegiate studies began in the areas of communications and physics. My small United Methodist college in Iowa, however, did not have a robust physics department. I worked closely with the professor to cobble together a minor by adding some independent studies and special projects.

One of these was a focus on cosmology: the forces holding our universe together, the stars and systems it contains, and how it all came into being. One day Dr. Olsgaard handed me a book called *God and the Astronomers*, by Robert Jastrow. What I remember clearly is the epilogue of this little book. It described the way scientists, physicists, and cosmologists have been climbing a mountain of knowledge and inquiry for centuries trying to discover ultimate truths about the origins of the universe. But when they get to the summit of this climb, what they find at the top are theologians who have been asking the same questions. I thought about the way Aristotle observed the heavens and determined there must be an "unmoved mover" and how some contemporary physicists find that the Big Bang points to God rather than contradicts Scripture. I read that passage in the book and discovered that in the shared quest for this answer, I wanted to be among the theologians rather than the cosmologists. My studies of the heavens were not about discovering who I was and where we come from. I wanted to understand the One who was behind it all. The next week, I became a religion major.

When I look up at the heavens, I do so with an immense appreciation for the mathematical genius that keeps it all spinning. The wonder of life is that we exist on a planet so perfectly placed nearly 92 million miles from a sun and that the forces of gravity keep us in this orbit. I think the heavens are declaring God's glory, and I want to listen to what they are saying. I want to appreciate the beauty of each sunrise and the wonder of every lunar eclipse not simply because of what they add to my life, but because they are gifts from the God who set the heavens in motion.

One of the traditional stories we tell during Advent and Christmas is about the journey of the magi from the East. They paid attention to the stars in the sky not just to observe their orbits, but to ask what the heavens had to say about the realities taking shape around them. And when a star appeared in the sky, they understood it to be a sign of great and wonderful things being born into this world. They allowed their scientific observations to lead them on a journey of faith.

What I love about the magi is that they come from a world in which science and religion are not strangers or polar opposites, but intertwined spheres of knowledge. Their journey to honor the birth of Christ reminds us that science can play a role in our expressions of Christian faithfulness. We can look up at the heavens and discover God's glory. The natural order and laws that govern life on this planet can lead us on a journey of faith when we discover something out of the ordinary. It can either be an opportunity for delight and praise or a realization of our need to repent and change our ways.

If the magi had been focused solely on their observation of the skies or solely on the sacred texts of the people of earth, they would have missed the connection. The new star in the sky would not have led them on their faithful journey so far away to honor the newborn King. We, too, are called to pay attention to our stories of faith and to the handiwork of God that surrounds us so that we can respond in ways that honor our Maker.

Creator of the stars of night, you called the magi to Bethlehem through a light shining above. Help us to observe and ask questions of the universe which we call our home, and lead us into action and care for your planet. Amen.

3

Christmas Trees in the Bayou

The whole creation waits breathless with anticipation for the revelation of God's sons and daughters. Creation was subjected to frustration, not by its own choice—it was the choice of the one who subjected it—but in the hope that the creation itself will be set free from slavery to decay and brought into the glorious freedom of God's children.

(Romans 8:19-21)

Another version of Clement Moore's famous poem, "The Night Before Christmas" is told down in Cajun country. As the clatter arises on the bayou, the narrator looks out to see what has caused the ruckus: "Cux dere on de by-you w'en I stretch ma'neck stiff, Dere's eight alligator a pullin' de skiff. An' a little fat drover wit' a long pole-ing stick, I know r'at away got

18

to be ole Saint Nick."[1] This Santa figure doesn't show up in a sleigh, but by boat! It's a uniquely Cajun take on a Christmas tradition.

Another unique aspect of the holidays in that region are the Christmas Eve bonfires that light up on the levees along the Mississippi River. While they may have had roots in the ancient practices of ritual fires to mark the solstice, the bonfires today help direct traffic along the river, guiding families to midnight mass and helping to lead Papa Noel to the homes of children.

When your home and your land and your life are built upon what it means to live on the water, that imagery tends to seep into your traditions as well—fires by the river, and alligators pulling Santa's sleigh. But what happens to these Christmas traditions when the waters along the coast in Louisiana rise? What happens to those impacted by climate change?

The delta that lies at the foot of the Louisiana "boot" is formed because the Mississippi River endlessly shifts and moves, depositing rich and fertile sediment and silt all along the way. However, as humans have sought to control the river and built up communities along its banks, dikes and levees were established to protect the people. We tamed the "Mighty Mississippi," but as a result we have altered Louisiana's coast. Land is disappearing because the Mississippi no longer deposits the amounts of soil it used to. Estimates from the United States Geological Survey show that southern Louisiana has lost nearly 1,900 square miles of land between 1932 and 2000.[2] People and communities who live here are becoming climate refugees, forced to flee from their homes. Children have to move away from these wetlands and rivers. Do they wonder how Papa Noel will find them?

Looking around at the world, signs like the disappearing bayou show us how the earth has been impacted by human activity and how we have fundamentally changed our environment. Our sin and greed, desire for stable land and comfort, all have caused us to make short-term decisions that have long-term consequences for the whole of creation— water, land, plant and animal life. As our focus Scripture for today reminds us, creation was subjected to frustration and it is trapped in the slavery of decay. Jesus warned that before the Human One comes again we would experience that groaning and breathless anticipation of creation: "There will be earthquakes and famines in all sorts of places. These things are just the beginning of the sufferings associated with the end" (Mark 13:8).

Historically, those wetlands served as a buffer for tropical storms and hurricanes, absorbing some of the energy and water. Now much of that land is gone. When Hurricane Katrina made landfall in 2005, the full brunt of the storm hit the land. The reality is that as the climate around us changes, severe weather events have become more common and more deadly. Their damages include dramatic changes to ecosystems and communities, the loss of life and property. The marks of devastation have lasting impacts. All the earth is waiting, breathless, longing for the new creation to be realized.

Paul believes God has linked the restoration of creation with the children of God, and that means we find hope in this season of Advent in the possibility that people of faith can help change the tides of decay. One small way that the people of Louisiana are working to protect and restore the wetlands is by collecting their used Christmas trees and dropping them into threatened bayous, where they become the basis for new marsh vegetation and collect sediment, reversing erosion. How can your Advent and Christmas practices help reverse the decay of our world in anticipation of Christ's renewal of all creation?

Holy God, forgive us for selfish actions that have changed this world we call home. This Advent, stir our hearts and transform us into your children. This world is waiting for us to take up our calling. May it be so. Amen.

---

1. TheCajunGaigin, "Cajun Night Before Christmas." Online video clip. YouTube, December 24, 2012. https://www.youtube.com/watch?v=1Vs2T_mhXfw. Text at http://www.findmall.com/read.php?52,1115060. Accessed May 11, 2017 and June 16, 2017.
2. "100+ Years of Land Change for Coastal Louisiana," https://www.nwrc.usgs.gov/upload/landloss11X17.pdf. Accessed July 19, 2017.

4

Contingency Plans

This is what God planned for the climax of all times: to bring all things together in Christ, the things in heaven along with the things on earth.

(Ephesians 1:10)

Every year in my church we have a Christmas cantata that our church choir puts on. For months we rehearse the music and practice the solos and learn the lines. Then, on the Sunday right before Christmas, the message of the cantata replaces the sermon for the day. The choir brings the good news of Christ's birth to the entire congregation in song.

This past year, however, there was the threat of bad weather on our Cantata Sunday. We knew this was a possibility, but there was also a chance that the system would fizzle out before it arrived. When I woke up early that Sunday morning, only a very light snow was falling. But it was falling on top of a thin layer of ice. More would be on its way as the morning would go on. I suddenly realized that we hadn't made a plan!

The thing about a plan is that it has a goal and a direction, and it contains contingencies. It prepares for all of the possible situations you can think of, and it sets forth what should happen in the case of each variable and at what time. The goal in our case would have been to put all of that hard work to use and to share the cantata with the congregation, no matter what. But we should have had a plan to make sure that was a reality: if the weather is fine, we have the cantata as scheduled; if there is a foot of snow, we'll postpone it to such and such a date; if we find ourselves unsure of what to do, these are the people who will make a decision that morning.

Churches around us were cancelling worship that day, but I knew that without a postponement date arranged ahead of time, it might be tricky to reschedule our big presentation. I quickly sent a text message to a few key people. After some back and forth, we decided to go ahead and present the cantata that morning. We urged people to use their best judgment and stay home if they felt it was unsafe to be out. Everything turned out okay, and we had decent attendance considering the conditions. But the morning filled me with stress and anxiety that simply didn't have to be there.

Next time, we need to have a plan.

As I look out upon this world, sometimes it feels chaotic. Although I believe that God created the heavens and the earth, you and me, it is hard to see the order and the purpose behind so many things that have gone wrong. Maybe that is why these words from Ephesians bring me so much comfort and hope. They are a reminder that God has a plan. The goal of this plan is to bring all things together in Christ, who John's Gospel tells us is the Word, the source of all that is (John 1:1-3). From the very beginning when this world was created, God's plan was put into motion.

That doesn't mean the path of this plan hasn't changed. After all, any good plan has contingencies. Although we turned away from God, God kept reaching back out to us. God made covenants with our ancestors. God rescued us from oppression. God called to us through the prophets. And then God came to us, became one of us, so that we might hear in a new way the story of why we are here.

During this season of Advent, we are invited to hear again about the plan set in motion before the stars were set in the sky. We pore over the words of the prophets, calling us back into right relationship with God and this creation. We immerse ourselves in the gospel narrative of how God so loved the world, the cosmos, that God's only Son was born into our lives. We also look forward to that day, at the climax of all time, when the goals of this plan will be accomplished. Advent reminds us that the day is coming when Christ will come again.

You are the Alpha and the Omega, the Beginning and the End, and all things are held together in you, O God. When we falter, help us to take comfort in your contingencies. And never stop calling us to align ourselves with your plan and purpose for our lives. Amen.

5

Wildfires

The LORD's messenger appeared to him in a flame of fire in the middle of a bush. Moses saw that the bush was in flames, but it didn't burn up. Then Moses said to himself, Let me check out this amazing sight and find out why the bush isn't burning up.

(Exodus 3:2-3)

As Advent begins, churches and families pull out the seasonal decorations, and our churches and homes are ablaze with light. My grandparents' house had a candle in every window this time of year. I fondly remember how we could pick out the house from blocks away as we drove in late at night. We light fires in our fireplaces and gather in the warmth of the flame to sing songs and cherish time together. And as the days get shorter, the Advent candles we light in worship are a sign that the Light of the world is coming to make all things new (Revelation 21:5).

As we prepare for Christ to come, we remember not only the birth of Christ, but also our longing for this world to be restored. In his sermon "The New Creation," John Wesley begins with everyday realities we experience, including forces and elements such as fire. He speculates on how God might redeem even these most basic parts of creation. That very fire we gather around this time of year, Wesley envisions as a destroyer. He talks of its power to dissolve virtually anything it contacts. Fire is both powerful and harmful. But fire is also life-giving, and Wesley says that in the new creation, "it will destroy no more: it will consume no more: it will forget its power to burn.... But it will probably retain its vivifying power, though divested of its power to destroy."[1] Fire itself will be redeemed as a pure force of life, not death.

As I hold in my heart that image of a life-giving flame that can no longer destroy, I think of the burning bush that pulled Moses out of his routine. God appeared in the midst of this fire and proclaimed the site as holy ground (Exodus 3:5), calling Moses to respond to the injustice and oppression of God's people. Moses would have missed the opportunity to respond if he hadn't paid attention to how the fire burned.

When I was a teenager, my church youth group worked at Yellowstone National Park on a mission trip. While there, we saw Old Faithful and other geothermal features like hot springs and acid pools. But just like Moses, I came across an amazing sight: a place where the bushes had burned. Only, in this case, wildfire had destroyed the forest. In the remains of blackened trunks and ash were also the brilliant greens of new life. Where once had stood majestic conifers, there now grew hundreds of small fir and pine trees. The contrast was breathtaking and strangely beautiful.

A sign read, "Naturally reseeded by wildfire." Wildfires are vital to the renewal of forests. But as the climate has changed, bigger fires, longer wildfire seasons, and far greater damage have disrupted the natural cycle where old growth and fallen trees are cleared to make room for new life. David Cleaves, a former climate science advisor to the U.S. Forest Service, notes that "if the area cannot regenerate, or we cannot get to it and reforest it, then it doesn't get back into the carbon sequestration and storage game as quickly as it would otherwise."[2] It creates a vicious cycle, because when these large fires burn, more carbon is released, fewer trees have the capacity to store the carbon, and the earth is likely to warm even more.

These wildfires are our burning bush, and we need to stop what we are doing and turn aside to discover what is happening in the flames. Not only do the flames have the power to destroy, but so do we ourselves as consumers of carbon-based energy sources like natural gas, oil, and coal. If the vision of the new creation is of a fire that no longer destroys, but only brings life, then our challenge this Advent is to consider how we might be people who no longer destroy the resources of this earth, but live in ways that are life-giving and sustainable. As the light of Christ shines in our lives, we can provide hope in the midst of creation's oppression.

Yahweh, you hear the cries of not only your oppressed people, but of your broken planet. You speak to us in the midst of the flames. Help us to live in ways that bring life rather than destruction upon this world. Amen.

1. John Wesley, "The New Creation," http://www.umcmission.org /Find-Resources/John-Wesley-Sermons/Sermon-64-The-New -Creation. Accessed May 25, 2017.
2. Quoted in Chris Mooney, "The Really Scary Thing About Wildfires Is How They Can Worsen Climate Change," *The Washington Post*, May 14, 2015, https://www.washingtonpost.com/news/energy -environment/wp/2015/05/14/how-massive-wildfires-can -actually-warm-the-planet/?utm_term=.f348c4d6c960. Accessed May 25, 2017.

6

All Creatures of Our God and King

He said to them, "Go into the whole world and proclaim the good news to every creature."

(Mark 16:15)

Every Advent and Christmas season, as I unpack our Nativity set and place the pieces on the mantle, I am reminded that the good news of God really was meant for every creature. My particular set comes with a donkey, two sheep, an ox, a goat, and a camel! Not only was the hope and promise of the Christ Child proclaimed to the creatures in the fields, but these creatures actively played a role in bringing Jesus into the world and welcoming him. We tell stories about how the donkey carried the very pregnant Mary to Bethlehem. The creatures gathered around the manger gave up their feeding trough for his bed. We hear about the shepherds in the field guarding the sheep, and when they hear the good news of the Savior's birth they rush into town. We always picture a few of those sheep, if not all of them, coming along for the journey. All of these creatures are as essential to the story of our faith as we are.

Today's focus verse from Mark is not found in all of our Bibles. The ending verses—everything after 16:8—are thought to have been later additions to the text rather than original to the story Mark was telling about the life, death, and resurrection of Jesus. So this command to preach "to every creature" may not have been part of Mark's Gospel originally. But we know that as that child in the manger grew and taught among us, he continued to point to birds and fish as signs of God's love and care and power. They were part of parables of care and providence, and they were the objects of miracles of abundance. And so it makes sense to me that as Christ leaves the work of carrying on the faith to the disciples, he would challenge them to care for every creature, to preach to every creature, to save every creature as a part of his final words before ascending to heaven.

In this Advent season, as we not only remember his birth but look forward in hope to the day Christ will come again, it is good for us to ask if we have been living out his words. Among the ancestors of our faith, one example of someone who took that call seriously is Saint Francis of Assisi. He never hesitated to proclaim the good news of God to any creature he met. Stories abound about how he spoke to animals and invited them to praise their Creator.

In one of these legends, Francis came upon a rabbit that had been caught in a trap. He gently released the rabbit and asked the creature to be more careful in the future. "Brother Rabbit, why did you let yourself be caught?" he asked. When he tried to let it go free, the rabbit kept coming back to sit on his lap. Eventually, another one of the brothers had to take the rabbit at some distance and release it, because it refused to leave Francis's side!

Francis was also known to release fish that had just been caught back into the waters. In one of these instances, he was being ferried across a lake when he received as a gift a very large fish that had just been caught. When he promptly put the creature back in the water, both the fish and the fisherman were surprised! Often, if he was preaching or telling stories about God while out on the water, fish would gather around and listen until Francis finished and he blessed them and dismissed them.

This Advent season, we remember that all beings have but one God, our Father and Mother, who cares for us all. Let us follow the example of Saint Francis and consider each creature our brother or sister in this journey of faith.

Lord of all creation, thank you for all the creatures of this world. Help us to remember that they are not only characters in our stories of faith, but that their hope lies in your love and new creation as well. Amen.

7

Mni Wiconi

Then the angel showed me the river of life-giving water, shining like crystal, flowing from the throne of God and the Lamb through the middle of the city's main street. On each side of the river is the tree of life, which produces twelve crops of fruit, bearing its fruit each month. The tree's leaves are for the healing of the nations.

(Revelation 22:1-2)

Our focus Scripture today lifts up one aspect of the new creation. We are told in Revelation that there will be a "river of life-giving water." Water is life. Or in the Lakota tongue, *Mni Wiconi*. And this isn't only a promise of the time when Christ will come again. In the words of the baptismal liturgy in my tradition, we remember how the Spirit of God hovered over the waters and brought forth light and life. We remember how we were saved through water in the days of Noah and led through the waters to freedom in the days of Moses. We tell the story of how Jesus was nurtured in the waters of a life-giving womb. We recall how baptism in the waters raises us to new life in Christ. Water is a symbol of the advent and the completion of our salvation. Water is life. Mni Wiconi.

Last year, as the temperatures dropped, the camps near the Standing Rock Sioux Reservation grew. Energy Transfer Partners were trying to lay a pipeline near the native lands in order to get oil from the Bakken fields to places farther south and east. An early route for the Dakota Access Pipeline was to cross just north of Bismarck, North Dakota; but when there were concerns raised, the route was shifted south. The new path would run under Lake Oahe near the reservation, crossing the Missouri River at that point. The river is a primary water source for those who live on the reservation, and many were protesting about potential contamination of their water.

Those who gathered at the camps were living out a calling to be water protectors and to cherish the life-giving waters of this creation. They believe that water is sacred. Mni Wiconi. I was moved again and again as I read stories of the protests at Standing Rock from colleagues and friends who journeyed to join in the efforts. One colleague told me about how he was struck by the prayerful and ceremonial atmosphere of the camp.

One of my Advent practices last year was to follow a series of devotions on Medium with a rather visceral title. The "PG" version was known as #rendtheheavens. The devotions sought to move away from feel-good spirituality during Advent and recover the bold, intense longing for God to show up that is also an undercurrent of the season. Throughout the series, themes of water quality kept coming back over and over. The various authors called upon people to cry out in laments to God because we hold in our hearts the vision of the new creation and because we are so far from that reality we simply can't stand it anymore. Each reflection lifted up current events that could lead someone to shout expletives as we long for the abundant life God desires not only for the people, but the whole planet. Come, Lord Jesus, was the daily cry.

Last Advent, I kept turning to the definition Archbishop Chaput gives for hope. He claims that it is choosing to trust in God while also noticing the realities of this world in an unfiltered way. He calls hope a discipline, and I believe we are invited to live out that hopefulness through action that enters into reality and embraces our call to truly be the children of God here and now.[1] Our Advent posture of longing materializes in a different way of life. We are people of the already but not yet, and we trust that God will use our lives today to bring the new creation into being.

Taylor Gould shared the call that woke her early on her first morning in the Oceti Sakowin Camp: "Sun Dancers, get up! Pipe carriers, get up! Christians, dust off your Bibles and get up! You are here for a reason! The black snake is getting near the river. Get up and do something!"[2] Christians who joined them were not only repenting of the abuse of the land and these native peoples, but also were putting their bodies on the line for the sake of the new creation. Advent holds before us that vision of life-giving water and invites us to turn our hope for its reality into action.

Life-giving God, you have placed in our hands the sacred task of caring for this creation. You are waiting for your children to rise to the occasion and claim the life you intend for us. May we protect the waters of life and share your hope with the world. Amen.

1. Archbishop of Denver Charles J. Chaput, "'On Christian Hope' and Advent," *Catholic News Agency*, December 5, 2007, http://www. catholicnewsagency.com/resources/advent/bishops-previous -advent-teachings/on-christian-hope-and-advent/. Accessed December 2, 2016.
2. Taylor Gould, "Standing Rock: Here for a Reason," *Inter.* http://inter. ifyc.org/-standing-rock-here-for-a-reason. Accessed January 29, 2017.

Week Two

Clearing the Way Through Stewardship

8

Keep Watch!

Nations and kingdoms will fight against each other,
and there will be earthquakes and famines in all sorts
of places. These things are just the beginning of the
sufferings associated with the end.

(Mark 13:8)

Advent calls us to be alert and to keep watch for the coming of the Lord. Even as Jesus walks among the disciples, he invites them to look ahead to when "they will see the Human One coming in the clouds with great power and splendor. Then he will send the angels and gather together his chosen people from the four corners of the earth" (Mark 13:26-27). We aren't just waiting for Jesus' birth. We are waiting for the time when Christ will come again to usher in the day of the Lord.

The disciples begin to ask questions about when this will happen, and Jesus describes signs that point to the beginning of the end. War. Earthquakes. Famine. Persecution. They all make the list. They all remind us that Christ is near and that the day will come. But these signs are not in and of themselves something to fear. They should not cause us to panic or turn toward false hope and fake saviors. Instead, we should keep watch and stay alert and redouble our commitment to the way of Christ.

Every generation can and does apply this Scripture to the reality of the world that surrounds them. When I look out at our world, I am aware of how energy resources like oil and gas have become the pivot point around war and conflict in the Middle East. Many of these power struggles have left people impoverished and starving. But some of these struggles are also connected with the way the climate is changing as a result of human activity. Studies have shown how extreme drought in Syria was a factor in the uprising that began in 2011 and has continued to destroy the country. In the United States, we are even faced with research that shows the extraction of these resources from the earth are causing the ground to shake. Small earthquakes associated with fracking are being felt from Ohio to Oklahoma to Pennsylvania.

There are some in the Christian faith who celebrate these signs of suffering and welcome the destruction of the earth and its peoples because it means Jesus will come back sooner to take us away from it all. Yet other Christians reject this perspective that cares so little for our earthly home and is content to ruin our air, soil, and water. The breadth of Scripture instead tells us that this is where God will bring about our salvation. And we are called to proclaim the good news of God for all of creation, standing firm in the life-giving promises of God in the face of the suffering caused by people of this world (Mark 13:9-13).

Rather than a call to disengage, sit back, and wait for Jesus, I think the thrust of this apocalyptic vision in Mark's Gospel is a call to engage and resist forces of destruction. Reading this passage during Advent reminds us of our call to be stewards and caretakers of this world. And if this is the job that has been given to us, then the last thing we want is to be found sleeping when Christ comes again (Mark 13:34-36). As people of faith, we can choose to reduce our consumption of these resources as a living witness that the good news of God is for all of creation. Anticipating Christ's birth and his return, we can work to lessen the effects of a changing climate and protect the people who have become the most vulnerable. As Mark's Gospel reminds us, this is our charge...even if it means putting our lives on the line.

Holy God, you call us to stand with your creation until the end of days. As the earth shakes around us, help us to not shrink in fear, but send your Spirit to help us choose another way. Keep us awake and alert for this task. Amen.

9

The Great Smog

The LORD God formed the human from the topsoil of the
fertile land and blew life's breath into his nostrils. The
human came to life.

(Genesis 2:7)

In the beginning, after God took the stuff of this earth and
formed us, God then breathed into us and gave us life. The
air all around sustains us, enables us to breathe in oxygen
and breathe out carbon dioxide. The Scriptures tell us that
this breath comes from God. The complex intricacies of our
respiratory system are astounding. The trees and the plants
around us "breathe," too. They are as much a part of the cycle
as we are, absorbing the carbon dioxide and releasing the
oxygen we need to survive.

Barbara Snyder reflected on what it meant to breathe in
this season of Advent: "gasping for a breath of the Divine /
longing for a birth of life to come in these moments / to bridge

the gap of here and now with infinite eternal."[1] When we read in Romans that "the whole creation waits breathless with anticipation" (8:19), it is not such a stretch to imagine all living things of this world holding their breath with excitement for the children of God to be revealed. All around us, the world is longing for the gap to be closed between our current reality and the promise of the new creation.

On December 5, 1952, a fog settled over London. The days had been bitterly cold and the coal fires in homes across the city were burning as high as they could. It was a deadly combination. As they burned the coal, people were filling the air with pollution, which stayed over London because warmer air above trapped it in place. When the toxic smog eventually lifted nearly four days later, estimates are that between four thousand and twelve thousand people had perished.

Scientists at Texas A&M have been looking back at the Great Smog of 1952 to try to learn what lessons it has for air pollution today. They discovered that the confluence of chemicals in the air created sulfuric acid above London.[2] Those pollution levels are comparable to the smog over cities today like Beijing and Mumbai, which have grown rapidly in terms of both population and industry. Studies done by Nanjing University have found that almost a third of the deaths in seventy-four cities in China (over one million deaths in a single year) could be linked to pollution.[3] One important voice we encounter during Advent, that of John the Baptist, challenges us to clear the way for the coming of God. I wonder if part of that means clearing the air, removing toxins and restoring breath and visibility so that we can encounter God freely.

You can be breathless with anticipation, but to be breathless also describes how air catches in your throat because of anxiety or stress. When our respiratory system doesn't work, or when the air around us is no longer safe, or when the trees are cleared away, all of those interwoven systems involved in our breathing break down. In Romans 8, creation is also "suffering" and "groaning," and the striving of verse 23 also points to the fullness of life that is missing when our breath is stifled.

If you search on the Internet for "time-lapse smog Beijing," you will find countless images and videos of how quickly the smog can roll into a city. But I am heartened by the reality that we can change our patterns of behavior. While it took a few years, England enacted the 1956 Clean Air Act and curtailed the causes of the toxic smog, making it safe to breathe again. We must remain vigilant and keep adapting our efforts to the latest technologies and dangers. Our role is to keep clearing the way for the life-giving breath of God in this world.

Breath of God, blow fresh into our lives. The world is gasping for your Spirit to fill us with new life so that we may have the resolve to clear the way for all to breathe freely. Help us to close the gap and usher in your new creation. Amen.

---

1.   Barbara Snyder, "Breathing Advent," https://merewhispers.wordpress .com/2013/12/23/breathing-advent/. Accessed May 26, 2017.

2. "Researchers Solve Mystery Of Historic 1952 London Fog And Current Chinese Haze," *Texas A&M Today*, November 14, 2016, http://today.tamu.edu/2016/11/14/researchers-solve-mystery-of-historic-1952-london-fog-and-current-chinese-haze/. Accessed May 26, 2017.
3. Josh Berlinger, Steve George, and Serenitie Wang "Beijing's Smog: A Tale of Two Cities," *CNN.com*, January 16, 2017, http://www.cnn.com/2017/01/15/health/china-beijing-smog-tale-of-two-cities/. Accessed May 26, 2017.

10

Lumps of Coal and Saint Nicholas

People were bringing children to Jesus so that he would bless them. But the disciples scolded them. When Jesus saw this, he grew angry and said to them, "Allow the children to come to me. Don't forbid them, because God's kingdom belongs to people like these children."

(Mark 10:13-14)

Coal and Christmas have long had a deep connection. Traditions from a number of different cultures talk about a gift-giver who brings joy and laughter to children. Many of these gift-giving tales also include warnings toward children who were naughty: they would get coal, sticks, or worse! Because several of these gift-giving figures got into homes through chimneys, coal, wood, and ashes would have been convenient to grab from the hearth and put into the shoes or stockings left to be filled.

One of the real people our traditional image of Santa Claus is based upon is Saint Nicholas. Nicholas was the Bishop of Myra in the fourth century, and he is known as a miracle worker. He used his wealth to help the poor, the needy, and the suffering. One story tells about how he secretly provided the gold needed for the dowry of a poor man with three daughters. He tossed bags of gold coins through their window secretly, where they landed in stockings that had been set by the fire to dry. His life of mercy and generosity exemplified the love of Christ for the children of this world.

The lump of coal Saint Nicholas leaves in naughty children's stockings is stored carbon formed from the transformation of ancient plants by time, heat, and pressure. It is extracted from the earth by miners who risk life and limb to provide heat and energy to homes across the world. Mining has always been a dangerous profession, and in December of 1907 two of the deadliest disasters in U.S. coal mining occurred. In a post commemorating the one hundredth anniversary of these tragedies, Christina Duranko notes that 362 lives were lost in Monongah, West Virginia, on December 6th. Another 239 tragically died in Van Meter, Pennsylvania, on December 19th in a separate accident. Though they happened on different dates, both occurred on the Feast day of Saint Nicholas in their respective communities.[1]

Saint Nicholas is highly revered by Catholic and Orthodox Christians, particularly those from Eastern Europe and

Russia. Depending on one's ethnic heritage, this feast day is celebrated on either December 6th or December 19th. In the early twentieth century, many immigrants living in the Eastern United States saw this date and Easter as the two most important holidays in the year. In Monongah, Saint Nicholas's day was celebrated on December 6. In Van Meter, it was celebrated on December 19. While the mining accidents in these communities were devastating events, the lives of many were saved because they had refused to attend work that day and had gone to church instead. As the headline in *The Pittsburgh Press* read after the disaster in Van Meter, "St. Nicholas Feast Saves the Russians." Many believed that lives were spared due to Saint Nicholas's intercession. That this intercession occurred not only once in December of 1907, but twice, is astounding.

Jesus tells us that God's kingdom belongs to the little children, and on the feast day of Saint Nicholas we are reminded of our call to protect the children of this world from exploitation and abuse, poverty and sickness. In many ways, we are praying for a miracle in the midst of a political climate around the globe that favors the quick and profitable extraction of this world's natural resources, no matter the consequences for the planet and the people. We balk at getting coal in our stockings, and yet we don't hesitate to dump mining waste into streams and rivers that eventually supply the water for children in rural Appalachian communities.

In a liturgy from Belgium that celebrates the life of Saint Nicholas, he is remembered as a "savior of people in distress, helper of the poor…opponent to dishonestly acting rulers, defender of innocent victims of corruption and misuse of power."[2] This Advent, we are called to be better stewards of God's creation and through better stewardship and care of our natural resources to protect this world for future generations. In the spirit of Saint Nicholas, we are called to take a stand against corporations and governments that cause harm to people and places. We should join in prayer that all who are responsible for our society might become like Saint Nicholas, acting with compassion for the vulnerable.

Thank you, God, for giving us not only the example of Christ, but the lives of people like your servant, Nicholas. Help us to act in ways that protect our children and our planet from greed and corruption, and help us to live with generous hearts. Amen.

1. Christina Duranko, "Darr Mine Disaster The 100th Anniversary of the Miracle of the Intercession of St. Nicholas," http://patheoldminer .rootsweb.ancestry.com/darr4.html. Accessed May 26, 2017.

2. "Prayer Service on the Feast of St. Nicholas," http://www .stnicholascenter.org/pages/prayer-service/. Accessed May 26, 2017.

11

Gifts for Our Children

I brought you into a land of plenty,
to enjoy its gifts and goodness,
but you ruined my land;
you disgraced my heritage.
(Jeremiah 2:7)

One Christmas, my extended family was all gathered together at my grandparents' house. We have a rather large family, but my young eyes noticed there appeared to be fewer gifts around the tree than normal. Grandpa Earl stood up and looked around at all of us, grinning, and announced that he and my grandma wanted to take the whole family on a special trip that year. It became the first of many vacations we would all take together to the island of Oahu, Hawaii.

My grandparents were successful in life, and as they thought about their legacy and heritage, they wanted to help all of us grow closer together as a family. They wanted to help us experience the beauty and joy of this world in a way we might not have been able to do on our own. Every few years as we gathered at Christmas time, they would stand once again and invite us to join them on a trip to paradise.

A Mennonite bishop once said that you begin to raise a child a century before it is even born, "because that's when you start building the environment they're going to live in."[1] In today's focus Scripture, Jeremiah reminds the people of Israel of their devotion to God as they became the "early produce of the harvest" (Jeremiah 2:2-3). God cleared the way for them to enter the land of plenty, where they were given everything they needed. In many ways, God was building the environment and the community for future generations. It was the Israelites' responsibility to share the space, resources, and the care for the land in gratitude.

But the temptation of humanity is always to want more. Israel pushed the boundaries of their territory and sought other gods. They forsook the living water and spent their energy and time digging wells that couldn't hold water (Jeremiah 2:13). A popular proverb teaches, "We do not inherit the earth from our ancestors, we borrow it from our children." The Israelites would have benefitted from such a warning. They wandered from God and destroyed the land and their children's heritage in the process.

That human impulse likewise impacted Hanauma Bay where my family visited. The bay was nearly destroyed by changes to open fishing laws in the 1950s and 60s. Families freely fished the waters, and marine populations were greatly reduced until the bay was designated a Marine Life Conservation District. The fish population grew 600 percent in the next sixteen years.

I loved our first trip to this sheltered coral reef and the amazing fish and coral we discovered just below the water's surface. But the bay was overpromoted and overused by tourists like myself. By 1988, there were three million visitors a year, who filled the bay with suntan lotion, fed frozen peas to fish, and trampled on the delicate reef, not to mention leaving behind waste in many forms. Without intervention, the bay might have been ruined for future generations. Thankfully, a new management plan limited use and created opportunities to teach guests how to care for the ecosystem. As the director of the park notes, "We saw the light before it was too late."[2]

This Advent, we have the opportunity to clear the way and build an environment that protects God's heritage as a gift for our children. What my grandparents gave me for Christmas over all of those years was not just a vacation, but a love for a people, a land, and a unique sense of stewardship. Too often, tourists drop in and indulge and abuse a place without ever coming to understand the richness of its land or the impact of their choices. The gift of being able to return again and again over these thirty years has allowed me to see the way our overuse of a place can threaten its destruction. Because of the wisdom of Hawaiians who believe that the land is not theirs to own, but to manage and care for, someday I will be able to take my grandchildren to experience it, too.

Awesome God, this world is filled with creations that take our breath away. Help us to honor you through how we appreciate them. Help us to experience them wisely. Help us to receive these gifts in a way that allows future generations to love them, too. Amen.

1. Dan Barber, *The Third Plate: Field Notes on the Future of Food* (New York: Penguin, 2014), 31–32.
2. Regina Gregory. "USA – Hawaii (Oahu) – EcoTipping Points at Hanauma Bay," http://ecotippingpoints.org/our-stories/indepth /usa-hawaii-hanauma-environmental-management.html. Accessed May 26, 2017.

12

Brown Water

Is feeding in good pasture or drinking clear water such a trivial thing that you should trample and muddy what is left with your feet?

(Ezekiel 34:18)

Shepherds and sheep are familiar images in the weeks leading up to Christmas. These are typically gathered in awe-filled adoration around Jesus' manger, or abiding in the fields just before the angels appear to them on the night Jesus was born. The shepherds represent the lowly in society, the very people Jesus came to stand with and among. Yet this chapter of Ezekiel reminds us that not all shepherds are faithful caretakers. In the prophet's message, God is sending a word of judgment upon the shepherds, the leaders of Israel. They were tasked with taking care of the flock and making sure that all in their charge were fed and protected, healed and loved—all of which they had failed to do. And not only does God promise to hold the shepherds accountable, but the sovereign Lord will also separate the "sheep and the goats" (34:17) in the flock, the lean and the fat sheep, the ones who created space for others and the ones who took all they could.

When Jesus describes what will happen on that day when "the Human One comes in his majesty" at the final judgment, he points back to this passage from Ezekiel (Matthew 25:31-46). As we wait in this season of Advent for Christ to come again, we are called to take these words of judgment to heart. We are called to turn our hearts outward toward others, especially those in our midst who are vulnerable. We are invited to repent of the ways in which we have forgotten to care for the flock. This year when you see the imagery of shepherds during Advent and Christmas, I invite you to remember that, today, you have the opportunity to choose a different way of being in this world.

Advent is typically a time when we think of others, when we give to those in need. Often we focus on individual acts of care, and we give our clothes and canned goods to relief organizations. We help build wells in remote places and visit people in prison. All of those are worthwhile causes, but in this particular Advent season, I want to challenge you also to think about the systemic ways that we trample the pastures and muddy the waters and have allowed entire flocks of people to be neglected. These verses from Ezekiel can be used to hold accountable the leaders in our nation and world who have focused more on their own interests than those of the people. What would it mean to provide for others in this way during Advent, focusing not on individual needs but on creating societies and communities that allow people to flourish rather than limit them or prey upon them?

Consider, for example, the city of Flint, Michigan. In 2014, the city had its water supplies diverted from the Detroit water system to one supplied by the Flint River. This was part of a plan to save money by the county through a new water authority, and plans had been worked up since 2012. But almost immediately, there started to be problems with water quality. Not only was the water more corrosive than it had been before, but bacteria were detected, prompting chlorine and chemicals to be added to the water supply. But this in turn created more problems and in January of 2015, residents were warned that the water contained substances that could cause health issues, including higher risks of cancer. In February of 2015, the levels of lead detected in the water by the EPA were seven times greater than healthy limits.

What amazes me about this story is that in October of 2014, the General Motors plant in Flint stopped using the city's water because the water was corroding its engine parts. But when the city tried to switch back to Detroit water in January of 2015, the emergency manager denied the request because of the costs. It took another year for the city to switch back to a different water source. By that time, the damage to the pipes was done and the entire infrastructure needed to be replaced. At this point, with lawsuits pending, and charges brought against at least nine government employees, the crisis is still not resolved and without filters the water is still unsafe to drink. Many don't even trust the filters.

Images from Flint that show the rusty brown water pouring out of faucets are heartbreaking reminders of the way the powerful muddy the waters for those in their care when they focus only on themselves. The resources of our world are meant for life, and yet those who are the most vulnerable are often the ones who bear the brunt of injustices. We can continue sending bottles of water to the residents of Flint, to give drink to those who are thirsty. But this Advent, we also remember our call to be stewards of the resources of this world and to ensure clear, safe drinking water for all people. Sometimes, that means holding accountable the shepherds when they fail us.

Holy God, we ask your forgiveness for when we have been so focused on ourselves that we turned away from those in need. Whether we are shepherds or sheep in the flock, help us to protect the vulnerable among us and to put their needs above our short-term benefits. Amen.

13

Acquiring More

Doom to those who acquire house after house,
*   who annex field to field until there is no more*
*   space left*
*   and only you live alone in the land.*

(Isaiah 5:8)

In Dan Barber's book *The Third Plate*, a farmer describes why rubber tires are forbidden for the nearby Mennonite community. "Rubber tires enable easy movement, and easy movement means that, inevitably, the farm will grow, which means more profit. More profit, in turn, leads to the acquisition of even more land, which usually means less crop diversity, more large machinery, and so on."[1] For the Mennonites, this represents being more and more removed from the land and less intimate with the soil they have been given to care for.

God judges endless profit and gain through the prophet Isaiah. The law required the people to leave gleanings in the fields and to care for the poor, but they consumed it all and stole from the poor (3:14). The leaders among the people in Judah rejected God and were no longer on the side of the widow and the orphan (1:23). They became so focused on wealth, success, and power that they lost their intimacy with the land, the people, and their God. As our focus Scripture tells us, they acquired more and more, throwing parties for themselves and never once caring for the people or what they grew. They became rotten with corruption and greed. The community was fractured and because of their evil, the land would be ruined.

But into that darkness and distress, God offers hope for the oppressed. "The people walking in darkness have seen a great light.... A child is born to us, a son is given to us" (Isaiah 9:2, 6). God promises that one will come who will redeem and restore the land. And as people who wait for the birth of the Christ Child, we are called to protect the poor and to protect the land from any who would destroy it for their own personal gain. One person who heard this call and gave her life to live it out was Sister Dorothy Stang.

Sister Dorothy was sent to Brazil to work with family farmers in the Amazon rain forest. Large-scale logging and ranching operations saw the land as an opportunity to profit and began to acquire more and more. The vast extent of their operations meant that they were not intimately connected with either the people or the land. They victimized local farmers and were destroying the forest. They could only see their profits and not the reality that this environment is home to half of the world's plant species and that much of the earth's fresh water runs through its roots.

And so the work of people like Sister Dorothy was to encourage sustainable farming techniques and to protect the rain forest. Her efforts caught the attention of the powerful landowners and she was named to a hit list. As the Sisters of Notre Dame de Namur tell her story, assassinations were a way the wealthy "eliminate opposition to the clear-cutting and burning of the forest... [and] those who empower and educate the peasants."[2] But Sister Dorothy did not cease her efforts and continued to fight for those being oppressed. On February 12, 2005, she was murdered. In the wake of the attention garnered by her death, the Brazilian president put under federal protection almost 20,000 square miles of land.

The consumerism that accompanies this time of year pushes us to seek whatever is new, bigger, faster, or more powerful... and we want to spend less to get it. Gadgets and tools that claim to make our lives easier fill every catalog and commercial space. We are tempted by the promises they offer, without ever taking stock of how disconnected we are from the land and the people who produce them. Yet, this Advent, let us remember the judgment against God's people in Isaiah and instead seek to live in ways that deepen our intimacy with creation and our neighbors. We can do so by advocating for the forests and streams like Sister Dorothy. Or we can slow down and scale-down, thinking in terms of what is sustainable like the Mennonites.

Mighty God, you want to establish and sustain your kingdom not only in our hearts but in this land. Help us to live and work in ways that protect the people and the resources you have given to us. Amen.

1.   Dan Barber, *The Third Plate: Field Notes on the Future of Food* (New York: Penguin, 2014), 32.
2.   "Expanded Story of Sister Dorothy Stang," Sisters of Notre Dame de Namur, http://www.sndohio.org/sister-dorothy/Expanded-Story.cfm. Accessed May 26, 2017.

14

Capsule Wardrobes

Then Jesus said to them, "Watch out! Guard yourself against all kinds of greed. After all, one's life isn't determined by one's possessions, even when someone is very wealthy.... Don't worry about your life, what you will eat, or about your body, what you will wear."

(Luke 12:15, 22)

When we think about being stewards of this earth's resources, we often forget about clothing. However, the quickly changing trends of the fashion industry have drastically increased the production of clothes and reduced the quality of these "fast fashion" items. As this season of Advent leads into Christmas, stores are promoting all of the "must have" garments and accessories for winter and spring. Children and adults alike will receive clothes as gifts. The documentary *The True Cost* claims that there are eighty billion new pieces of clothing made every year, which is 400 percent more than twenty years prior.[1] Four hundred percent! Many of the pieces today are designed to be disposable; they are cheaper, but also lower quality, and we are more likely to throw them out when they wear out or go out of fashion. Each year, the average American creates eighty-two pounds of textile waste.

Planet Aid (planetaid.org) tries to prevent those clothes from ending up in landfills by recycling textiles, and they educate the public about the environmental impact of our clothes. A cotton shirt, for instance, can take up to 700 gallons of water to produce, which is "enough for one person to stay hydrated for 900 days."[2] They also note that when we throw away our clothes they can take up to forty years to decompose; a pair of shoes can take as long as a thousand years!

The quest for fashion is often about status and keeping up with trends. We think brands say something about who we are. One Christmas, I begged my grandparents for a Starter jacket, though I didn't care about football, but because everyone else had one. Yet, this is absolutely contrary to the message of the gospel. Jesus tells the disciples in Luke's Gospel that our lives are not defined by our possessions but by how generous we are with our living. The only status symbol that matters is the faith we build in God's kingdom.

As I have reflected upon the privilege and abundance that I truly have, I am almost ashamed by how much I worry about what I'm going to wear on any given day. One way I have tried to clear out this worry in my life is to minimize my closet with a capsule wardrobe. This is an intentional effort to limit your closet to thirty-three or fewer high quality, versatile items.

One of the tips offered up by *The True Cost* website is to ask the simple question: Will you wear it thirty times?[3] In a capsule wardrobe, every item can and should be worn at least once a week if not more frequently.

I reduced my closet by about two-thirds and donated items that were in good condition to a local thrift store. I have discovered that while I was overwhelmed before by too many choices, now every item has a purpose and getting dressed is stress-free. I don't have the temptation to endlessly shop, but I carefully consider how a new item might fit with the rest of my closet. And because each item is integral, I find I take better care of the individual pieces, taking the time to launder properly and mend when necessary. I used to throw out a pair of shoes when they wore out; now I take them to be repaired.

This week, our focus has been upon how we clear a way for God's kingdom in the midst of the clutter and distraction of consumer consumption by being better stewards. Too often, our possessions do become a source of worry and anxiety in our lives that distract us from the work of the Kingdom. That is why Jesus invites us to remember the lilies (Luke 12:27). When the messenger of God cries out to "clear the LORD's way" in Isaiah 40, it is a reminder of the temporary nature of our lives and the everlasting love of God. The grass will dry up and wither (Isaiah 40:7), yet still God provides (Luke 12:28). So our focus should not be on these temporary things that distract our hearts and harm the earth. Instead, let us long for God's kingdom.

God of the lilies, you ensure even the grasses of the field that are here today and gone tomorrow are dressed in beauty. Clear away our worries over status and possessions so that we can be more mindful of your creation and focus our eyes on your coming Kingdom. Amen.

1. The True Cost, http://truecostmovie.com/learn-more /environmental-impact/. Accessed May 26, 2017.
2. "8 Little Known Facts About Our Clothing Habits," *Planet Aid*, http:// www.planetaid.org/blog/8-little-known-facts-about-our-clothing -habits. Accessed May 26, 2017.
3. The True Cost, http://truecostmovie.com/learn-more/buying-better/. Accessed May 26, 2017.

Week 3

Discovering Joy
in the Abundance
of the Earth

15

Paved Paradise

You visit the earth and make it abundant,
enriching it greatly
by God's stream, full of water.
You provide people with grain
because that is what you've decided.
Drenching the earth's furrows,
leveling its ridges,
you soften it with rain showers;
you bless its growth.
You crown the year with your goodness;
your paths overflow with rich food.
Even the desert pastures drip with it,
and the hills are dressed in pure joy.
(Psalm 65:9-12)

John Wesley speculated on how God might recreate basic elements, like water, when Christ restores all of creation. He envisioned the air will be calm and "no more disturbed by storms and tempests." In many ways, Wesley was pointing back to the paradise of the garden in Genesis. There, the land remained fertile despite the fact God had not yet made it rain upon the earth (Genesis 2:5-6). The soil itself and its capacity for retaining water and providing for growth is truly amazing. Wesley imagines a paradise restored with waters "rising here and there in crystal fountains, to refresh and adorn the earth."[1]

As the daughter of a farmer, I have always appreciated a wet winter. When I was growing up, this was the time of year when we could start praying for rain or snow. We wanted the moisture to hold off until all of the harvesting was complete and the equipment had been put away. But when that was done, our longing for a white Christmas was as much about the soil as it was the magic of waking up to a winter wonderland.

Sure, April showers will bring May flowers, as the old adage goes, but the soil has the ability to retain water and sustain growth through entire seasons. Even in temperate climates with long, dry summers, a wet winter can provide moisture for growth all year long. As our psalmist reflects upon the way God provides growth through the rain, his words remind us not only of the precipitation, but also how the furrows and ridges of the earth will drip with joy . . . starting with the rain and snow of winter.

I must admit, however, that whenever I think of "the earth's furrows" I picture the freshly tilled soil of the spring and the cuts of the plow that break up the snow-covered ground. There are benefits to spring plowing, like incorporating manure or disrupting weed growth, and breaking up the surface of the soil increases the temperature and makes it easier to plant. But when we alter the furrows and ridges of the earth, we also increase the risk of soil and water erosion. The precipitation the earth had been storing during the wet, winter season is exposed.

Altering the furrows and ridges of the earth is something we are all complicit in. We are constantly building, excavating, and changing the landscapes around us through sprawling urban areas, mall parking lots, and the roofs of our houses. As Joni Mitchell put it in her song, *Big Yellow Taxi*, we've "paved paradise and put up a parking lot." No matter what we have built, the rain and snows fall. And all of these paved, hard surfaces inhibit the quenching waters of the sky from replenishing the soil in our communities. Instead, we are forced to use on-demand water supplies like the hose in your backyard or irrigation systems to bring life to the plants around us.

Part of our Advent longing is for the renewal of paradise in the new creation. Until that day, the rain and the snow are how God enriches the soil of the earth. One way we can joyfully serve God and this planet is by seeking ways to support the natural water-retention capacity of the soil, so that we might experience God's abundant blessings.

There are a number of ways that you and I can turn away from "paving paradise" and can help make sure the furrows and ridges of the earth are able to absorb all of the blessings of God. In many urban areas, green roofs are being planted that allow plant life to soak up rainfall, rather than letting it run off. In your own yard, a rain barrel connected to your downspouts can capture water for later use. Or, you can work to add organic matter, like compost, to increase the water retention capacity of your lawn or garden. All of these efforts help the earth rejoice, filled with the waters of life, dancing, shouting, and singing.

Earth-Tamer, Ocean-Pourer, the blessing of water fills this earth and brings forth life. Thank you for the abundance you bring to us, even when we don't deserve it. Help us to enrich this earth and appreciate its growth. Amen.

---

1. John Wesley, "The New Creation," http://www.umcmission.org/ Find-Resources/John-Wesley-Sermons/Sermon-64-The-New-Creation. Accessed May 31, 2017.

16

Jubilee

You will plant your fields for six years, and prune your vineyards and gather their crops for six years. But in the seventh year the land will have a special sabbath rest, a Sabbath to the LORD: You must not plant your fields or prune your vineyards.

(Leviticus 25:3-4)

On the weekend after Thanksgiving, the Christmas tree goes up at my house. We carefully unpack each ornament and hang them on the branches, plug in the lights, and flip the switch. And then, the tree slowly and gently spins. We have our artificial tree set on a mechanical base. It rotates without tangling up any cords or decorations, and it always feels magical.

Once the tree is up, one of my favorite things to do in the evenings is to sit on my chair and watch it spin. Captivated by the twinkling, I get to take the time to appreciate every ornament and the memories they carry with them. They mark moments of my childhood, friendships, my marriage to my husband. Some call to mind the bright and shining faces of our nieces and nephews and things they have made. I can be still for hours, resting by the tree's light and finding joy and delight in everything that God has provided.

Those quiet moments of rest are mini-Sabbaths in the midst of a busy holiday season. They fill my life with gratitude as I remember where I have come from and how I have been blessed by God with an abundance of relationships that sustain my days. None of it has been the work of my own hands, but every person and every memory is a gift from God.

That is the joy of Sabbath. Every seventh day God calls us to Sabbath rest, and every seventh year we are to let the land lie fallow. We are to cease our working and our striving and simply bask in the provision of the Lord. That means no work in the fields, no planting or pruning, and no intentional harvest. Fundamentally, the Sabbath in Leviticus 25 reminds the people that their ability to use the land, to be fed from its soil, is not a right, but a gift.

In many ways, this was a jarring command. The ancient Israelites had just escaped slavery in Egypt, and soon they were told that once they finally had land they must take a year off without reaping its benefits. It must have been a scary thought. Yet this practice was intended to remind them of their dependence upon God, and it was for the benefit of the land itself, allowing the earth and its creatures to rest and replenish. One result is that all of creation would experience God's abundant provision and presence.

Later in Leviticus, Moses proclaims that every fifty years there would be a special Sabbath of total restoration. Not only was the land given rest, but the people were called to release the slaves and cancel outstanding debts. This vision of Jubilee, the Day of Reconciliation (Leviticus 25:9), is proclaimed by psalmists and prophets as they wait for the birth of the Messiah who would bring God's salvation and presence to all people.

I need those moments of quiet rest by the Christmas tree to still my heart and to help me refocus on why we gather to celebrate. It is far too easy to get caught up in the fervor of the holidays and to spend money on gifts and food and décor until our credit cards are stretched to their limits. We do so in the name of Jesus, but forget that the one who is about to be born among us came to forgive debts and bring rest and renewal to our world.

As Jesus began his ministry, he read from Isaiah, "He has sent me to preach good news to the poor, / to proclaim release to the prisoners / and recovery of sight to the blind, / to liberate the oppressed, / and to proclaim the year of the Lord's favor" (Luke 4:18-19). And so, as we prepare for his birth, let us be people of the Jubilee, taking delight in rest, easing the burdens of others, and celebrating the gifts of God that sustain us every single day.

Awesome God, you provided for your people in the Sabbath years and you provide for us every day. Fill our hearts with jubilation as we receive your gifts of renewal and life, and help us to pass them on to others. Amen.

17

Justice and Joy

Let heaven celebrate! Let the earth rejoice!
Let the sea and everything in it roar!
Let the countryside and everything in it celebrate!
Then all the trees of the forest too
  will shout out joyfully
  before the LORD because he is coming!
He is coming to establish justice on the earth!
  He will establish justice in the world rightly.
  He will establish justice among all people fairly.
          (Psalm 96:11-13)

My husband and I have eight nieces and nephews between the two of us, and we love them dearly. When we visit at the holidays, we are overwhelmed by the excitement of their anticipation. Little fingers pull back curtains to peer out and catch a glimpse of us as we arrive. We barely shut the doors on the car before we begin to hear the commotion inside the house as they clamor to be the first to greet us. When the door finally does open, little bodies leap into our arms giving hugs and kisses.

Those joyful moments as they anticipate our arrival are nothing compared with our anticipation of the birth of Jesus and his return. We remember how when Mary visited her cousin Elizabeth, the yet-unborn prophet John leaped for joy in his mother's womb (Luke 1:41). So great is the joyful waiting of Advent that the whole earth is on pins and needles waiting for God's revelation of justice. As the Message translation captures the jubilation, "Let Wilderness turn cartwheels, / Animals, come dance, / Put every tree of the forest in the choir" (Psalm 96:12 MSG).

We are not simply waiting for a person to arrive on our doorstep, but longing for the fullness of life that the Lord will bring. We know God desires wholeness for all people and all parts of this creation. The thrust of the biblical story reminds us that justice and restoration are on their way.

Like our nieces and nephews who excitedly gather, look out the windows in anticipation, and leap into action at the first hint of our arrival, we are called to prepare for the birth of Christ in an active way. As the people of God, we have been given a part to play in this story: "to do justice, embrace faithful love, and walk humbly with your God" (Micah 6:8).

In her hymn, "For Everyone Born a Place at the Table," Shirley Erena Murray invites us to create space for other people to experience the wholeness and love of God. While the lyrics talk more about our human community, our focus verse for today reminds us that the earth, too, waits expectantly for justice and restoration and wholeness. These realities are interconnected and "God will delight when we are creators of justice, justice and joy."[1] We can create, enhance, and support justice for all parts and peoples of this world through the choices we make every day.

Today, the intersection of environmental concerns and disparities among various communities highlight the need for environmental justice. Vulnerable populations have been impacted by climate change-related drought and flooding that have reduced their ability to sustain their lives through farming. Everything is interrelated, from the availability of quality water, to the loss of biodiversity, to trade agreements that keep prices so low growers cannot afford to purchase their own products. It altogether leads to intense disparity between the poor and wealthy of the planet.

As we prepare to welcome our coming Lord and his reign of justice, let us consider how our decisions impact our relationships with one another and the creation that sustains us. We are tasked with working toward wholeness and justice throughout the world. And that means we should try to support efforts that bring hope and joy and abundance to all people and places.

This Christmas when we head home, my husband and I will bring gifts in celebration of the birth of Christ. My prayer is that the things we choose will not only bring joy to my nieces and nephews, but can also bring justice and joy to the families who produced them and to their corner of the planet.

Whether it is choosing to purchase fair trade chocolate, coffee, or nuts; making a donation to support farmers in vulnerable communities; helping girls access water in their villages; or up-cycling things we might have thrown out, you and I can make a difference in this world.

The sky and the earth, the sea and the land are shouting your praises, God, for you are coming to bring justice to all people and places. Help us to join in the chorus with acts of justice and joy that honor you and your creation. Amen.

---

1. Shirley Erena Murray, "For Everyone Born A Place at the Table," © 1998 Hope Publishing Company.

18

Poinsettias and Dirt

He existed before all things,
and all things are held together in him.
(Colossians 1:17)

The season of Advent is a stressful time to be in ministry. Not only are you personally trying to deck the halls and make Christmas plans with your family, but you are also coordinating all of the special events at church that come along with the season. You simultaneously need to ensure that presents get purchased, everyone's favorite hymns get sung, and none of the multitude of bulletins have typos. It can feel like "all things are held together" through the work of a handful of staff and volunteers, and yet those who gather on Christmas Eve will only see the end results of all that work.

A few of the churches I have been a part of have a tradition of changing the seasonal poinsettia decorations from red to white for Christmas Eve services. One year we forgot to make the change, and there was a mad rush to switch the sanctuary's plants about an hour before worship. In the process, a few poinsettias fell, spilling dirt all over the altar carpet. We pulled out the vacuum, repotted the plants, and no one was the wiser.

Luckily, our Advent chaos is temporary. We don't have to hold all things together all the time. While we are called to produce fruit for the Kingdom, the truth is that we only do so because we have been strengthened by God. That child in the manger is also the first over all creation, and all things in heaven and earth were created in Christ. By him alone is it all held together, and all things exist through the Son—from the stars in the sky to that dirt that spilled on Christmas Eve.

In many ways, the life of Christ that sustains us is like that soil, giving life and support to all so that the world might bear fruit. We think about dirt as dead matter, but in reality it is organic, full of life. Without dirt, life as we know it would cease. One gram of fertile soil contains somewhere around a billion bacteria, and they consume what is produced by green plants. Our soil is filled with fungi that decompose materials and other creatures that consume, decompose, and feed on one another. Those creatures also leave tunnels in the soil, which increase the infiltration of minerals, water, and oxygen. And all of these living organisms live off of and feed off of one another.

Fred Magdoff describes it this way: "'To me there is real beauty in how it works,' he said. 'When there is sufficient and varied food for the organisms, they do what comes naturally. . . . What you have is a thriving, complex community of organisms.'"[1] It is the interaction of all of these things, held together, that makes our soil healthy and good. God desires all parts of the body to function together with Christ as the head (1 Corinthians 12; Colossians 1:18). Like our churches, with many people working together for God's glory, the soil thrives on diversity, and embracing it allows abundance to fill the earth. Every part of creation is essential to the health of this planet, and it is all held together through Christ. Sometimes our churches fail to appreciate the gifts of our members, or we compete with one another. Likewise, the actions we take in our agricultural and economic systems can undervalue the importance of every unique organism. We are willing to strip out the diversity God has given us in the soil for the sake of convenience and production.

The busyness of Advent in a church is made manageable when we encourage all parts of the church to work together and play their part to create something beautiful, mysterious, and powerful. In the same way, we can joyfully honor the soil beneath our feet. In your own back yard you can plant beneficial plants together or rotate which plants you put where each season to help your soil thrive. We are rediscovering that when we provide for the soil, the soil provides for us. It is part of this creation, held together in Christ, to bring glory to God in this world. So much of this world sustains our life without ever being seen, but it all works together to bear abundant fruit. Including poinsettias.

Invisible God, we are quick to strip away differences, and we think unity means that everything looks the same. Help us to find joy in the diversity of this world you hold together, even in the dirt beneath us. Amen.

---

1. Dan Barber, *The Third Plate: Field Notes on the Future of Food* (New York: Penguin, 2014), 86.

19

Seeds of Kindness

Then God said, "I now give to you all the plants on the earth that yield seeds and all the trees whose fruit produces its seeds within it. These will be your food."

(Genesis 1:29)

While some families use things like "Elf on a Shelf" to encourage good behavior in their children during this time of year, the folks at the blog *The High Calling* have started an Advent practice around seeds of wheat. Their family sets out a few small pots filled with dirt, and they challenge their children to practice acts of kindness as they wait for Jesus to be born among us. For each one, they get to plant a tiny grain of wheat. On Christmas Eve, they trim the shoots that have sprouted forth and place them in the manger of their Nativity scene. Throughout Advent, they have been creating the "hay" for the bed of Jesus through their actions. It is a reminder that simple acts can change the world, or as the author poetically puts it, "Just this seed unfurling, impossible power contained in the small."[1]

Advent reminds us of the power contained in the small seed. We spend these weeks waiting for the birth of Jesus, the very bread of life (John 6:35). In doing so, we remember that it was Mary who, through the simple act of saying yes to God, allowed that seed of life to be planted within her. Likewise, the kindness of Joseph, shepherds, and wise ones helped abundant life to enter the world.

We also wait for Christ to come again and usher in the Kingdom that he told us was like a mustard seed. It is merely a tiny seed when it is planted, but will grow to bless the world (Matthew 13:31-32). That Kingdom has already been planted in our world through the birth of Jesus Christ, and it is growing all around us. Every day we have the opportunity to be a steward of its growth and to increase its abundance through our acts of love and kindness.

This has been our job from the beginning. In Genesis 1, as God set all of creation in order, God blessed us with food from the plants of the earth. In that simple act, everything we needed to experience abundant life was placed at our fingertips. By not only tending the plants, but also harvesting, saving, and sharing the seeds, we ensure future generations would taste their fruits. Each and every seed brings sustenance and life and multiplies its blessings year after year.

And yet, much like we forget to nurture and pass along the good news of Jesus and the kingdom of God, we have not always cared for the seeds that give us life. We have lost countless varieties of plants due to poor management, natural catastrophes, or war. Once the seeds are lost, the species is gone forever. Organizations like Seed Savers Exchange remind us of our role as caretakers for not only the seeds of the earth, but also for one another. Such organizations encourage gardeners and farmers to send in their seeds for sharing with the world. Their farm now stewards over 20,000 plant varieties.

About five years ago, my sister-in-law wrapped up as my Christmas gift a few paper envelopes filled with tiny seeds. Each one had been grown in her own garden the year before, and she saved the seeds from a few plants. There were Black Krim and Yellow Pear tomatoes, Chives, and King of the North peppers. It was a simple act of love and kindness that filled my heart with joy. I carefully planted seeds of each variety and labeled them, waiting breathless for them to sprout and bear fruit. They did! I have continued saving their seeds, filling my garden with their abundance and passing along seeds, plants, and fruits to friends and family ever since.

An act as simple as saving a seed from a tomato or pepper and passing it on can help make sure the abundance of God is known by all by preserving the diversity of our food supply. Our acts of kindness help the coming reign of God take root and spread to all people. And in doing so, they lovingly create the manger on which Jesus will lay his head.

Creator God, you not only gave us seeds for sustenance and life, but you entered our lives like a seed, hidden in the womb of Mary. As we steward the seeds of the planet, may we also steward the seeds of your Kingdom. Amen.

---

1. "One Small Seed: When Wise Men Decide to Do Advent," *The High Calling,* https://www.theologyofwork.org/the-high-calling/blog /one-small-seed-when-wise-men-decide-do-advent. Accessed May 31, 2017.

20

Breaking Bread

You make grass grow for cattle;
*   you make plants for human farming*
*   in order to get food from the ground,*
*   and wine, which cheers people's hearts,*
*   along with oil, which makes the face shine,*
*   and bread, which sustains the human heart.*
                                        (Psalm 104:14-15)

As my husband and I were growing up, neither of our families ate a lot of meals around a table. We were the start of the generation tempted by endless sports and arts activities, and both of our families juggled it all with two working parents' schedules. It seemed like we never had all of the members of the family home at the same time. Everyone grabbed whatever they could, whenever they were home. Even the big family holiday dinners we experienced with extended family rarely happened around a table because there simply were too many of us! We crowded in around folding tables, with others carefully balancing their plates on their knees on couches and recliners.

I have since learned to create space for things like breaking bread and sharing cups of wine with friends and family around a table. Maybe that is because my call to ministry was formed around a table in the tiny basement chapel at Simpson College where we celebrated weekly Communion. We gathered around a circular table and as we broke bread, we could look into the faces of all who were present. You could feel the love and grace and peace in the room. The bread we shared was lovingly baked every week by Patty LaGree, whose husband Kevin is a United Methodist pastor and at the time was the president of our school. The bread was nutty and sweet and hearty, and it crumbled a little bit in your fingers. We became an intimate, holy, close-knit family.

My first church appointment was to a small town in eastern Iowa, and it was close enough that we could drive every Friday night to my sister-in-law's house for dinner with her husband and children. At 6:00, we'd walk in the door and be greeted with gigantic hugs and shouts of joy. We'd place our offering for the meal, usually warm garlicky bread, on the table and we'd all sit down to dig in. The kids fought over who got to sit by whom. We'd tell stories and giggle. Everyone proudly explained what they made for the meal . . . especially my nieces and nephews who were learning all sorts of things in the kitchen.

The family dinner table is one of the most powerful analogues we have for what it means to be the people of God.

As we gather around the table, we gather with often familiar faces for a familiar taste of grace. We sing those same old songs and tell our stories. We feel warm and comfortable and welcome. Each person contributes as a part of this body of Christ that is formed there. We celebrate and give thanks to God for all of the ways we have been formed and forgiven and blessed.

Psalm 104 is a litany of the ways our Creator God has provided for this world. It describes the place for everything and everything in its place, from the donkeys to the stork to the sea creature Leviathan. Everything is made with wisdom, and the psalmist also points us forward to that moment after our deaths when the breath of God will "make the surface of the ground brand-new again" (104:30). In the middle of it all are human beings. God provides grain and wine and oil, our focus verses tell us, "to make people happy, / Their faces glowing with health, / a people well-fed and hearty" (104:15 MSG). These core elements, lifted up in the psalm, do more than simply feed our bodies. They nourish our souls. While the lions might gather in their dens, we are meant to be with one another, and joy is found in shared meals.

Today my husband and I live in a different city, but Friday night dinners have remained a part of our life. Only now, friends and their families gather around our table. We crowd in, pull up chairs, and feast on the offerings of bread, oil, and wine. When I look around at the faces full of joy and laughter, brought together by such simple gifts from the earth, I catch a glimpse of the coming reign of God.

Bless the Lord, O my soul! You established this earth and provide for every corner and creature. And you have provided for me. Help me to find joy in the simple gifts of this earth and the deep ways they sustain life and community for me. Amen.

21

Candied Carrots

Why spend money for what isn't food,
and your earnings for what doesn't satisfy?
Listen carefully to me and eat what is good;
enjoy the richest of feasts.

(Isaiah 55:2)

About this time of year, the holiday parties start to fill up our calendars. I can remember one year in particular where I had seven different Christmas events to go to in about forty-eight hours. Each gathering is typically filled with food: sweet, fatty, salty, delicious food. This is a time for feasting, celebrating, and remembering the reason for the season.

When Isaiah, the prophet of the Lord, invites everyone to a feast, it isn't just any party . . . no, this is the promise of the heavenly banquet. When Isaiah envisioned this day of salvation, he wrote about "a rich feast, a feast of choice wines, / of select foods rich in flavor, / of choice wines well refined" (25:6). Now Isaiah brings word that all who are hungry and thirsty should turn from their ways and come to the table. Life and life abundant is waiting for all who seek the Lord.

And so, as we celebrate the birth of Christ into our midst, we gather around tables with friends and family to feast. Our gatherings are a glimpse of that heavenly table, and I'm sure that every person, in every culture, imagines a different sort of spread. We all have those favorite dishes that warm our souls and make us feel like we are home, and so naturally we picture them somewhere in that feast.

I know that for me, the holidays just aren't the same without candied carrots. We take a bag of humble carrots from the grocery store, slice them up, and slather them in a pot with brown sugar and butter until they are fork-tender and delicious. And yet, in many ways, we are spending money for things that don't truly satisfy. We do all of this work to our carrots to make them taste better by adding sugar instead of allowing carrots to grow in a way that allows them be naturally sweet and flavorful.

I personally hadn't thought much about this dilemma until I connected our focus Scripture alongside a chapter from Dan Barber's book, *The Third Plate*. Barber's goal is to grow food that tastes as good as it possibly can. One afternoon his vegetable farmer, Jack, came running in with a bunch of carrots that had just measured a Brix reading of 16.9. This measurement is used often in winemaking, but as Barber explains, it "also indicates the presence of healthy oils and amino acids, proteins, and—

this is key—minerals.... The carrots were 16.9 percent sugar—and bursting with minerals."[1] And they tasted like it!

To compare, Barber pulled out some of the carrots from the fridge that had been purchased for his restaurant. They measured a Brix reading of zero. There was absolutely no sugar or minerals in the industrial carrots. That's because those carrots you and I buy in the grocery store are designed to grow big, fast, and uniform. To create consistency and efficiency they are often grown in sand, with water and fertilizer added as needed, not in soil full of nutrients and minerals and microorganisms to feed the carrots.

As Isaiah issues the invitation to the feast, he calls the people to abandon the ways they fill their lives with things that don't really satisfy. He begs them to listen to God and to seek what is good and life-giving. For too long, we have thought that abundance in agricultural production meant quantity. We have allowed ourselves to be content with cheap produce, grown in bulk, without ever asking if we were getting what we have paid for. And then we are forced to supplement our diets with chemicals and pills in order to replenish all of those healthy minerals and vital nutrients we no longer get through our food.

In the season of Advent, Isaiah calls us to seek another way. God has already given us this earth, and it is full of abundance. As we prepare for Christ to be born in our midst, let us turn our attention back to the soil and allow the gifts of this earth to take root. When we do so, we will discover the richest of feasts.

Holy God, you have set a feast for us and call us to come and eat its riches. Lead us back to the abundance of this land with celebration as we turn from what doesn't satisfy. Thank you for every good thing that grows in this earth. Amen.

---

1. Dan Barber, *The Third Plate: Field Notes on the Future of Food* (New York: Penguin, 2014), 81.

Week 4

The Peace of the World's Creatures

22

Consider the Monarchs

Consider the ravens: they neither plant nor harvest, they
have no silo or barn, yet God feeds them. You are worth
so much more than birds!

(Luke 12:24)

At the front of the sanctuary in my congregation are two
gigantic, twelve-foot-tall Chrismon trees. It takes a crew of
about twelve to put them up, along with the wreaths we hang
along the walls and the blue Advent banners. This past year,
we got courageous and changed the color of the ribbons and
the balls that decorate their branches, but the one thing we
probably won't ever change are the Chrismons themselves.
They were hand-stitched by members of the congregation
years ago. They not only hold the symbols of our faith, but also
represent the faithfulness of generations past.

One of my favorite Chrismon symbols is that of the
butterfly. Maybe that's because it seems so surprising to find

it on a tree at the beginning of winter. Typically, we associate butterflies with the new life of spring and the promise of resurrection. But that itself is the reason it has a place among the other symbols. For what else is Advent but a longing for the new life of God to come?

Saint Francis remembered the teachings of Jesus and was moved by God to preach to the birds when he came across a tree full of them one day. As a child, I remember distinctly one fall when monarchs migrated through my front yard. Our trees were literally covered with butterflies, and I will picture that sight forever! Much as God moved Francis toward the birds, God has moved my heart toward the monarchs.

Our focus verse for today might seem out of place for a story about butterflies, but I've been concerned about how vulnerable our butterflies are, especially monarchs. Jesus invites the disciples to "consider the ravens" and to remember that God provides for even small and fragile creatures on this planet. When I consider the monarchs, I see that their habitats are filled with wildflowers that bear nectar for food. Milkweed provides food for larvae. Trees, especially firs, provide shelter, warmth, and protection.

God has also provided directions for traveling south. There are many birds that migrate to other climates as the seasons change, but the monarch butterfly is the only butterfly that makes a two-way migration. While spring and summer monarchs typically only live a few weeks, the ones that emerge in late summer or fall have an important job to do. They will live up to nine months and will travel south, often about a hundred miles in a day, to overwinter in Mexico. While they come from many places, their paths typically converge somewhere in Texas for the remainder of the journey to Mexico.

Yet that life cycle is threatened by the loss of habitat, increased use of pesticides, and a changing climate that impacts migration patterns. Dr. Lincoln Brower is a biologist who has spent his lifetime studying monarchs and has attempted to get them classified as a threatened species under the Endangered Species Act. "The monarch is the canary in the cornfield, a harbinger of environmental change that we've brought about on such a broad scale that many species of pollinators are now at risk if we don't take action to protect them," he argues.[1] Brower has observed that the winter colonies now only occupy a tenth of the land they had two decades prior.[2]

Saint Francis encouraged people to scatter seed along the roads for birds on Christmas Day so that all of God's creations might celebrate the birth of Jesus Christ into this world. In this season of Advent, my heart turns toward ways that we might help the monarchs to celebrate with us the coming of Christ as well. One of the simplest things we can do is to plant wildflowers and milkweed in our gardens, creating way stations that passing monarchs might use to lay eggs that will develop as larvae. In that way, we might bring peace and prosperity to one of God's threatened creatures.

God of birds and butterflies, not one creature escapes your notice or your care. You would seek to provide, and so often we have stood in the way of provision. May we embrace even the most delicate of your insects and share with them your peace.

1. "Monarch Conservation," http://monarchlab.org/monarch -conservation/. Accessed June 6, 2017.
2. Lincoln P. Brower and Homero Aridjis, "The Winter of the Monarch," *The New York Times*, March 15, 2013.

23

Beasts of Burden

Rejoice greatly, Daughter Zion.
  Sing aloud, Daughter Jerusalem.
Look, your king will come to you.
  He is righteous and victorious.
  He is humble and riding on an ass,
    on a colt, the offspring of a donkey.
                    (Zechariah 9:9)

I was printing up coloring pages for the children in worship as we prepared for the fourth Sunday of Advent. Our Scripture that day highlighted the journey of Mary and Joseph to Bethlehem, and it was a tangible image for our young ones to latch on to. A quick Google search of "Mary Joseph travel Bethlehem" yielded tons of great line drawings…and in every single one of them, Mary was riding on a donkey. Luke doesn't include this detail in his Gospel (Luke 2:4-5), but it has become such an integral part of the way we tell this story. Why do we assume this was the case even though no donkey is mentioned in the Bible?

There are a number of references to the ways donkeys serve as beasts of burden in our Scriptures. Moses put his wife and children on a donkey as they went to Egypt to set the Israelites free (Exodus 4:20). Abraham loaded a donkey with wood for the fire of sacrifice as he took Isaac up the mountain, only to have God provide in another way (Genesis 22:3-6). But I think above all, as this journey of Mary and Joseph leads them so close to Jerusalem, we see the impending birth of the King of kings in light of words like those of the prophet Zechariah.

We typically turn to this verse as we recall the triumphant entry into Jerusalem (Matthew 21:7; Mark 11:7; Luke 19:35; John 12:14). In its symbolism, we are reminded that Jerusalem rejoices because the king has returned in peace. This is not the entrance of a conquering general who has come on a horse to destroy, but a symbol that the time of war has ended and peace is among the people once again. As the Holy Family find themselves in Bethlehem, they are a mere five miles from the gates of Jerusalem. Rejoice, Jerusalem, your king has come!

In this verse from Zechariah and others in Scripture, we are reminded that the donkey is a simple, humble beast of burden. This creature serves a purpose, whether that is to be ridden or to carry goods, to thresh, or to plow. As Moses lays out laws and guidelines for living as God's people in the twenty-fifth chapter of Deuteronomy, a short verse stands out: "Don't muzzle an ox while it is threshing grain" (Deuteronomy 25:4).

Oxen, donkeys, and other beasts of burden would have been used in the threshing and grinding of grains from the harvest. Typically, they would have been yoked in order to turn a grinding millstone that would crush the grains into meal. The thrust of this verse reminds us that even creatures deserve to enjoy the fruits of their labors, and to muzzle an animal to prevent it from eating the grains that it was grinding would be cruel.

Just because an animal has been called upon to work does not mean that it is any less an honored part of God's creation. In each of the Scriptures mentioned above, God used these creatures to help bring about the end of oppression, the promise of hope, the return of peace. In the new creation, God will ensure that not only humanity, but all of God's creation experiences the fruits of that work.

John Wesley laments over the suffering of the brute creatures, in particular the beasts of burden, in his sermon, "The General Deliverance." "What returns for their long and faithful service do many of these poor creatures find?" he asks, eventually turning to speculation in the light of God's unending grace and love.[1] He envisions the peace of God transforming and redeeming all present suffering that humanity has inflicted upon the animal life of this planet. We are waiting for the day that not only Zion and Jerusalem, but all of creation will rejoice in the peace of God. And as we wait, Wesley calls upon all people to imitate the mercy of God and "enlarge our hearts towards those poor creatures."[2]

God of all gentleness, the creatures of this world serve your purposes as they provide and carry and work for the people. May we echo your gentleness in our care for the beasts of burden in our lives and help them experience the fruit of their labors. Amen.

1. John Wesley, "General Deliverance," II. 6, http://www.umcmission
    .org/Find-Resources/John-Wesley-Sermons/Sermon-60-The-General
    -Deliverence. Accessed June 6, 2017.
2. Ibid., III. 10. Accessed June 6, 2017.

24

While Shepherds Watch Their Flocks

Know your flock well;
pay attention to your herds,
for no treasure lasts forever,
nor a crown generation after generation.
When the grass goes away, new growth appears,
and the plants of the hills are gathered,
then the lambs will provide your clothes,
and the goats will be the price of your fields.
There will be enough goat's milk for your food,
for the food of your house,
and to nourish your young women.

(Proverbs 27:23-27)

Of all of the people in or surrounding the town of Bethlehem on the night of Jesus' birth, the angels appeared to the shepherds. While the rest of the town slept they were vigilant, watching over their flocks and protecting them from danger. Those humble and lowly shepherds out in the field were the first to hear the good news of the birth of the Messiah.

In my years of ministry, I have learned a lot about what it means to be a shepherd because our biblical stories are filled with pastoral imagery. One of the things I have discovered is that there is a drastic contrast in how we raise animals in the modern Western world and how those shepherds of Bethlehem would have cared for their flocks. We tend to raise animals for a singular purpose—either for meat or for milk—and large-scale operations (and confinement operations) are the primary sources of our food. In the ancient Near East, however, the shepherd personally led his flock. As he walked, the sheep would walk with him. Wherever he went, they would go. And so it is likely that when the angels appeared in the heavens that night over Bethlehem, the shepherd would have been awake, his body lying across the entrance of the fold to keep his creatures safe.

Many of the cuisines of the world developed from what the land of the region supported holistically rather than the farmers trying to meet the demands of the market as they do today. Like the proverbs wisely suggest, these people understood their flocks well and understood that the well-being of their herds meant the well-being of their families. The scale of production was much smaller, and many regional cuisines developed with more grains and vegetables than meat on their plates because the whole environment fed the people. They thought about how the grass and the lambs, the wool and the milk, the manure and the fig and olive trees all were intertwined with one another.

During this Advent season, as we gaze on that pastoral vision of the shepherds and their flocks, maybe we should pay attention once again to how the herds were tended. How can we truly care for the flocks in a way that ensures sustainability beyond this generation?

Chef Dan Barber is asking those questions. His restaurant, Blue Hill, is not only farm-to-table, but it was actually built on his farm. It was not too long, however, before Barber began to realize there was a problem with even his efforts. They were taking such wonderful care of their flocks and their pasture, moving the sheep to the freshest spots, letting chickens fertilize the land. It was the work of husbandry and shepherding and the spirit of the proverbs. Yet when the first lambs were ready for the table, he observes that "we had sold out in the time it takes to eat a hot dog."[1]

The problem with the way we eat today, especially in restaurants, is that we give the biggest chunk of our plate to the protein. We simply cannot eat this way forever. As we seek to live as people of the kingdom of God, we remember that our call is not simply to provide for our own bellies today, but to care for all parts of this planet. As we seek to steward and shepherd all of creation, one simple choice we can each undertake is to remember the three Rs: reduce, refine, and replace. We can reduce our portion sizes and eat less meat. We can refine our choices and choose proteins that come from well-cared-for animals. And we can replace some of the protein in our diet with more vegetable-based sources.[2]

The Kingdom we anticipate at Advent is a reality in which we live peaceably with all creatures, cherishing the life and food they give us, rather than seeing them only as a hunk of meat that fills our holiday plates.

Good Shepherd, we give you thanks for the flocks that feed our families. We pray that as we anticipate your Kingdom, we might also choose to eat in ways that pay attention to the lives of the creatures that sustain us. Amen.

1. Dan Barber, *The Third Plate: Field Notes on the Future of Food* (New York: Penguin, 2014), 13.
2. Allen Yeh "Animals and a Theology of Creation Care" *The Humane Society*, April 1, 2010, http://www.humanesociety.org/news/news/2010/04/creation_care_allen_yeh_040110.html?referrer=https://www.google.com/. Accessed June 6, 2017.

25

Peace for All Creatures

On that day, I will make a covenant for them with the
wild animals, the birds in the sky, and the creeping
creatures of the fertile ground. I will do away with the
bow, the sword, and war from the land; I will make you
lie down in safety.

(Hosea 2:18)

In the season of Advent 2015, we truly prayed for peace. The world around us felt like it was being torn apart by violence, with terror attacks in Paris, bombings in Beirut, marketplace shootings in Nigeria, and attacks in San Bernadino and Savannah in the United States. All of these attacks took place within a few weeks, in the midst of the season when Christians gather to light candles of hope, joy, and peace.

But that difficult season was also a reminder that our longing for the Messiah has always been a longing for peace. When his son John was born, Zechariah sang out, "Because of our God's deep compassion, / the dawn from heaven will break upon us, / to give light to those who are sitting in darkness / and in the shadow of death, / to guide us on the path of peace" (Luke 1:78-79). When Mary sang out the Magnificat, she was recognizing that the child in her womb was the answer to the longing of generations of people who had been lowly and oppressed (1:46-55). When the arrogant and proud are scattered, it will be because God's strength has been shown, not humanity's (1:51).

Perhaps that is because for far too long, our inclination has been toward violence. In the first chapter of Genesis, we find a paradisiacal vision with a vegan diet for all; no animal products are consumed by humans or creatures (Genesis 1:29-30). By the time we get to the fourth chapter, however, humanity has been kicked out of the garden, and one of the first sons offers up an animal as a sacrifice (4:2-4). Only verses after the first taking of animal life in the Scriptures is the taking of the first human one. Cain kills his brother Abel out of jealousy.

By the ninth chapter of Genesis, humanity has been devoured by sin and God wipes the slate clean with the Flood. Through Noah, both humanity and animal life is preserved by the building of an ark. When the waters recede, the meal plan is adjusted. "All of the animals on the earth will fear you and dread you. . . . They are in your power. Everything that lives and moves will be your food" (9:2-3). Hunting, fishing, and trapping are all blessed and sanctified by the Lord . . . as long as we honor the life within each creature and use it wisely.

This can be done in a way that truly appreciates the gift of life and the sacrifice of the creature. My husband and I have been watching a series on the History Channel called *Alone*. Ten participants are dropped off in remote and extreme wilderness locations with only a backpack full of gear, their wits, and a set of cameras. Foraging and gathering are important, but so is trapping and fishing. As each participant pulls in his or her catch, you can see the gratitude on their faces. Many say, "thank you" to the life they hold in their hands. They take care not to waste any part of the animal, but use the bones and guts for broth. They appreciate the sacredness of the meal.

We might not hunt for game with our bare hands, but we can be aware of how the protein we eat gets to our tables. We can pause for a moment of grace and be grateful for the meals that are set before us. We can seek the peace of all creatures—human and animal alike. After all, it appears that our ability to be so cavalier with the life of a creature pushes the envelope of our capacity to hurt one another.

When God promises the restoration of his people in Hosea, it is a vision of peace for all creatures...and that means our diet must change, too. As Matthew Scully notes in his book *Dominion*, a key idea throughout the Bible is "the way of peace toward man and beast alike, bringing closer the promised age when there is no more bloodshed and no more death."[1] This Advent, let us pray for that reality to draw near.

Holy God, after the Flood you set in the clouds your bow, a symbol of the covenant and a reminder of your enduring covenant of life with all creatures. Prepare us, O God, for the day when we, too, will set aside our bows and live in peace. Amen.

1.   Matthew Scully, *Dominion: The Power of Man, the Suffering of Animals, and the Call to Mercy* (New York: St. Martin's Press, 2003), 28.

26

The Friendly Beasts

The wolf will live with the lamb,
*   and the leopard will lie down with the young goat;*
*   the calf and the young lion will feed together,*
*   and a little child will lead them.*
The cow and the bear will graze.
*   Their young will lie down together,*
*   and a lion will eat straw like an ox.*
A nursing child will play over the snake's hole;
*   toddlers will reach right over the serpent's den.*
They won't harm or destroy anywhere on my holy
mountain.
*   The earth will surely be filled with the knowledge*
*   of the LORD,*
*   just as the water covers the sea.*

*   (Isaiah 11:6-9)*

My grandparents put out a number of Nativity sets at Christmas. Only one of them, however, was appropriate for little hands to touch and hold. It was placed underneath the Christmas tree, on the floor, where we could reach it. I remember countless hours of play by the tree, moving the little figurines here and there, making up adventures. I'm also fairly certain other characters and animals ended up in the scene as well—action figures, Sesame Street guys, and more barnyard animals than you could properly fit in the crèche.

But as I look back on the way we as children played with those molded pieces, I can't ever remember us including a predator in our display. The friendly beasts that surrounded that tiny baby—the Lamb of God—were always gentle creatures. Cows, pigs, donkeys, sheep, camels, zebras, and elephants...but never a lion, tiger, or bear. Perhaps even at a young age, we understood the danger of certain animals and couldn't imagine that it would be safe to include them at the birth of our Savior.

And yet, the longing of Advent is for that day when predator and prey might lie down in safety. The birth of that precious Child in the manger ushers in the peaceable kingdom where leopards and wolves would be perfectly suitable companions for calves and oxen. Isaiah's vision calls us to set aside our fears and to seek a future where no creature will bring harm to another.

I am reminded of a story from the life of Saint Francis. A village was being terrorized by a wolf that had eaten livestock and had killed a shepherd. The mayor of the village sent three strong guards into the woods to kill the wolf. Only one returned, and he told of how fierce and deadly the wolf was. The village grew more fearful. Desperate for help, the mayor asked Francis of Assisi to come, having heard Francis could talk to animals. Francis noticed the entire town was on edge, full of grief and desire for revenge. The peace of the village had been disrupted. He listened with an open heart and went to bed praying for wisdom.

The next morning, Francis went into the woods. From far off the wolf approached, and their eyes locked on one another. But Francis did not allow himself to become afraid. "Come, Brother Wolf, I command you in the name of Christ to do no harm to me or to anyone else." The wolf stopped, sat down, and listened. Francis told the wolf about the fear of the village and the harm he had done. He listened as the wolf told him that he had been abandoned by his pack and was scared and starving. He hadn't intended to kill the shepherd protecting the sheep or the guards; he was only defending himself.

God showed the monk that the answers lie in reconciliation and kindness. Francis could see the hunger and remorse of the wolf and suggested that if the wolf would stop killing humans and other creatures, the villagers would feed the wolf all his days. The wolf was afraid, but willing.

They returned to the village, where the people heard Francis's proposal. They discussed and recounted their own grief and fear, but with Francis praying and guiding them they found compassion for the wolf. They welcomed the creature as their brother, and the widow of the shepherd was the first to bring Brother Wolf food. Hate and fear lifted from their hearts, and the wolf and the village lived in peace until his death.

Isaiah shares a vision of the peaceable kingdom and of the coming day when the wolf and the lamb and the child will live in peace and no harm will be done any longer. As we wait this Advent for the Lamb of God to be born in our midst, ushering in that Kingdom, we are called to live into its reality through kindness, compassion, listening, and forgiveness. Someday, all creatures will find peace and safety near the manger of our Savior.

Lamb of God, you have shown us a different way of being in the world: one that begins in love rather than hate, in mercy instead of judgment. May this way of peace fill our hearts as we encounter all whom we might think of as enemies. Amen.

27

Children of Snakes

The LORD God said to the snake,
"Because you did this,
    you are the one cursed
        out of all the farm animals,
        out of all the wild animals.
    On your belly you will crawl,
        and dust you will eat
        every day of your life.
I will put contempt
        between you and the woman,
        between your offspring and hers.
    They will strike your head,
        but you will strike at their heels."
                (Genesis 3:14-15)

Last Advent, my Bible study group reflected on the peaceable kingdom from yesterday's devotion. Advent is, after all, a longing for the birth of the child who will bring this reality into being. Our discussion focused on the verse that describes how a toddler and a snake will play together when we dwell with God (11:9). One of the couples started to chuckle and told how their granddaughter had just put on her jammies when a shriek came from her room. A three-foot-long snake had made itself comfortable between her sheets. Parents came to the rescue and tossed the snake outside, and they spent hours trying to discover where the hole in the house might be. They had no intention of living peaceably with snakes.

Our animosity toward these creatures goes all the way back to Genesis. We were called to "take charge of the fish of the sea, the birds in the sky, and everything crawling on the ground" (Genesis 1:28). But we were tempted by the snake, who claimed that we could be like God (Genesis 3:5), and we committed an act of selfishness, striving for personal gain. Consequences ensued for both humanity and the snake. Enmity, contempt, strife became the new norm. In his book *Dominion*, Matthew Scully argues that mistreatment of animals amounts to an abuse of human power. He investigates the ways that our power, our dominion, has been used over, rather than for, other creatures:

> Animals are more than ever a test of our character,
> of mankind's capacity for empathy and for decent,
> honorable conduct and faithful stewardship. We are
> called to treat them with kindness, not because they
> have rights or power or some claim to equality, but
> in a sense because they don't; because they all stand

unequal and powerless before us. Animals are so
easily overlooked, their interests so easily brushed
aside. Whenever we humans enter their world, from
our farms to the local animal shelter to the African
savanna, we enter as lords of the earth bearing strange
powers of terror and mercy alike.[1]

Too easily, we lash out at other people and the animals of
this world not simply out of contempt or fear, but also from
a banal denial of the value of God's creatures. Like the snake
in the garden, we are full of justifications for our actions and
tempted to think only of ourselves. Perhaps that is why when
John the Baptist shows up preaching repentance in our Advent
Scriptures, his favorite put-down is "children of snakes" (Luke
3:7). He was sent by God to prepare the way for the ministry
of Jesus, and a great many people came out to hear his words.
His message was simple: "Produce fruit that shows you have
changed your hearts and lives" (3:8). He was calling them to
abandon the selfish roots of sin and to demonstrate love and
compassion. John knew, however, that like a snake filled with
poison, the hearts of many were still filled with sin.

We need Jesus Christ to be born into this world and to usher
in the kingdom of God because we have become the "children
of snakes." God intended us to take charge over the creatures
and show mercy and care. At our best, we demonstrate this
kind of love and companionship with our pets, but too often
we fail to notice the rest of God's creatures. The test of our
character is whether we can once again embrace our capacity
to know, love, and obey God and to share God's blessing

with all creatures. Let us hear the call of John the Baptist and prepare for the coming of the Messiah by producing the fruit of repentance. Then, perhaps, snakes and toddlers can truly play together.

God of the adder, our fears and insecurities cause us to use our power in ways that deny the life of other created beings. Forgive us for our misuse of power and help us to live in humility and love, seeking the peace of all creatures. Amen.

---

1. Matthew Scully, *Dominion: The Power of Man, the Suffering of Animals, and the Call to Mercy* (New York: St. Martin's Press, 2003), xi-xii.

28

The Wisdom of Children and Creatures

But ask Behemoth, and he will teach you,
the birds in the sky, and they will tell you;
or talk to earth, and it will teach you;
the fish of the sea will recount it for you.
Among all these, who hasn't known
that the Lord's hand did this?
In whose grasp is the life of every thing,
the breath of every person?

(Job 12:7-10)

One of my churches held an impromptu pageant every Christmas Eve. Our church was filled with older members who had grandchildren and great-grandchildren visiting, and a well-planned service was impractical. Instead, we had a variety of simple costumes available, and as families arrived the children chose who they wanted to be. Our box of costumes was filled with an assortment of creatures. Sometimes we weren't sure what the costume was meant to be, and the kids made up their own: cats, unicorns, lions, you name it. Everyone came to the pageant. During the children's moment, the whole "Nativity" would gather and the altar was filled with barks, bleats, and roars from the children.

I'm not sure many people listened to the sermon on those evenings. We were captivated by the innocence and exuberance of the children as they shared in the wonder of welcoming Jesus into our world. Dressed up as God's creatures, they taught us what it meant to know God's love and power.

In the Book of Job, we find a man who has had everything taken from him (Job 1:13-22). Many of his friends tried to explain the mysterious and unknowable nature of God, but Job pointed to how even created beings like birds and fish know that everything is held within God's hands. All we need to do is pay attention to what the creatures have to say. They were a testimony to the power of God over Job's life. And they continue to testify during this season of Advent. They remind us that all the earth is waiting for Christ to bring about the restoration of the earth. They are a living witness to the hope, stewardship, joy, and peace God brings to this world.

Ann Voskamp writes of a woman seeking a sign of hope during a difficult season, and the woman imagined that the bright blue color of the wings of a butterfly might offer it. The wings of the blue morpho butterfly are blue only on the top, and they have to be photographed in mid-flight at just the right moment to capture the color. After a long time of searching, waiting, and picture-taking, the woman had nearly given up. Her camera's battery nearly depleted, she started to leave. But then a blue morpho butterfly landed on her friend's shoulder and rested with its wings open—an exceedingly rare event. Looking at the bright blue wings, she exclaimed in joy, "How can we ever not hope in impossible things now?"[1] A butterfly became a witness of hope.

While we attempt to find a way to responsible stewardship, we might learn from animals that repurpose waste to make their homes. Australian bowerbirds collect colorful, discarded plastics to create structures called bowers to attract mates. They show us a way to transform garbage into relationships.

Elephants in the wild are known to "cry tears" of joy. When two separated elephants are reunited, they run toward each other trumpeting. They click their tusks together, flap their ears, rub their bodies together, and give loud, exuberant expressions of happiness. It reminds me of the joy we might experience when we reunite at the heavenly banquet.

Some animals also express altruism and protect other species. Humpback whales have been seen defending other animals, such as grey whale calves, that had been attacked by killer whales. In an act of sacrificial love, they are willing to use their energy and risk injuring themselves to protect even members of a different species. Perhaps they teach us how we might practice dominion and provide peace to others.

Meister Eckhart wrote, "Every single creature is full of God / and is a book about God."[2] In the same poem, he went on to say that he'd never have to write a sermon if he just spent enough time with such creatures, even those as small as caterpillars. As we await the birth of Christ into this world, we remember that the Word became flesh and that God took on the substance of all created life. In the Incarnation, Jesus became a part of the wholeness of creation—man and beast alike. As we wait for Christ to be born in our midst, let us not forget to seek him in the creatures of this earth.

Creating God, you speak to us not only through the words of the Scriptures, but through the life of your creation. Open our eyes and our ears to your story in plant and animal life, and help us to seek for them and for us the shalom of your Kingdom. Amen.

1. Ann Voskamp, "When You're This Close to Giving Up Hope," http://annvoskamp.com/2013/12/when-youre-this-close-to-giving -up-hope/. Accessed June 6, 2017.

2. Meister Eckhart, *Earth Prayers from Around the World: 365 Prayers, Poems, and Invocations for Honoring the Earth*, edited by Elizabeth Roberts and Elias Amidon (San Francisco: HarperSanFrancisco, 1991), 251.